PUBLISHER'S NOTE

In 1958, to celebrate Minnesota's centennial, the
Women's Division of the Minnesota Statehood Centennial Commission published this cookbook of
recipes gathered from kitchens throughout the state.
The cookbook was enormously successful, quickly
selling out two printings. When the commission was
disbanded, members arranged for the book to be
placed with the Minnesota Historical Society, which
has made it available continuously since then.

This best-selling book of favorite regional recipes is
now also a piece of Minnesota history. It is reprinted
as it was originally written and published, reflecting
the social conventions of its time and containing some
now-outdated references to ethnic groups and historical events. The accuracy of the recipes remains un-
changed, however, and *100 Years of Good Cooking:
Minnesota Centennial Cookbook* continues to delight
both cooks and their families.

CONTENTS

INTRODUCTION

Minnesota families have many wonderful heritages, and among the most cherished are the recipes which have been handed from generation to generation. The Women's Division of the Minnesota Statehood Centennial Commission is proud to be the sponsor of the Minnesota Centennial Cook Book, *100 Years of Good Cooking.*

The Women's Division is grateful to the many individuals and groups participating in this commemorative project. Special thanks go to the Centennial Women's Division county chairmen who coordinated the gathering of recipes in their respective areas; to the hundreds of women who individually submitted family favorites, and to the Minnesota Press Women who initiated the search for recipes. We are grateful, too, for the counsel of the Minnesota Statehood Centennial Commission staff in the preparation of this publication.

The National Secretaries Association of Saint Paul deserves special commendation for volunteering to type the recipes for printing—a very major contribution.

Appreciation goes to Jean James Baron, who authored the county facts and legends, and Joyce Schultz, Forest Lake, who sketched the inside illustrations.

The women of Minnesota are grateful to Virginia Huck and Ann Andersen, the editors who edited the recipes, selected the cover design and art work, and supervised the two thousand and one details necessary to publication.

Katy Heng

MRS. DONALD J. HENG
GENERAL CHAIRMAN

May 11, 1958

FOREWORD

The first thing you will discover about the Minnesota Centennial Cook Book, *100 Years of Good Cooking*, is that the recipes are practical and easy to follow. Grandmother had to cope with recipes which vaguely instructed her to "take a handful of sugar and the butter left from breakfast." We know you will appreciate the fact that all pioneer recipes included in this Centennial cook book have been modernized through the years by constant use in Minnesota kitchens. We are indeed grateful to the hundreds of homemakers who were generous enough to share these century-old family recipes.

We would like to have published every recipe submitted. Because of the wonderful response to the request for recipes, this became impossible. However, a heartfelt "thank you" goes to everyone who took time to submit a recipe, and, in some cases, who even baked a sample cookie or cake to send along.

The editors felt that a Minnesota Centennial cook book should highlight each of the state's 87 counties. Therefore space has been devoted to recipes from each county and a bit of fact and legend has also been included which we hope will add to your enjoyment of the cook book.

HERE'S TO GOOD EATING . . . with *100 Years of Good Cooking!*

V. H. and A. A.

May 11, 1958

AITKIN COUNTY'S forests still abound with game, as they did when the Lake Mille Lacs area was an Indian headquarters. Today, the legends of that past persist. Some say the ghosts of Indian warriors who died in battle come back to the lake to whisk, sighing, among the trees at night. Maybe, maybe not. But in the lake are many fish.

Avocado Salad Ring

4 cups mashed avocados (about 6)
4 tablespoons lemon juice
3 tablespoons gelatin
½ cup cold water
1¼ cups hot water
2 teaspoons salt
¼ teaspoon sugar
¼ teaspoon pepper
2 tablespoons onion juice
¾ cup mayonnaise

Mash avocados, sprinkle with lemon juice. Soften gelatin in cold water; dissolve in hot water; chill until it begins to thicken. Blend gelatin mixture with avocado, salt, pepper, sugar, and onion juice; chill until thickened. Beat 3 minutes, blend in mayonnaise; pour into 8½" salad mold and chill 2 or 3 hours. Unmold and garnish with lettuce leaves and fill center with sour cream shrimp dressing. Makes 10 to 12 servings.

Sour Cream Shrimp Dressing

1 clove garlic, halved
1 cup sour cream
½ cup catsup
2 tablespoons Worcestershire sauce
1 tablespoon grated onion
1 tablespoon lemon juice
1 teaspoon salt
½ teaspoon dry mustard
½ pound shrimp, halved

Rub small mixing bowl with cut surface of garlic. Pour in cream and add all ingredients except shrimp. Stir until blended, add shrimp. Place in refrigerator until ready to serve. Serve with avocado ring.

Shrimp Stuffed Green Peppers

1 teaspoon salt
3 cloves garlic
6 medium-sized green peppers
½ cup raw rice
1 can cream mushroom soup
  Juice 1 lemon
  Dash pepper
  Paprika
2 tablespoons grated onion
2 tablespoons butter
1 pound fresh cooked or
  2 5-ounce cans shrimp
1 teaspoon parsley, chopped
1 cup grated Swiss cheese
6 pats butter

Put salt and garlic into pan of 2 quarts of water. Bring to boil. Cut tops off peppers and scoop out insides and clean. Boil peppers 10 minutes. Boil rice. Put mushroom soup in sauce pan and add lemon juice, pepper, onion, and butter. Heat until butter melts. Add rice and cleaned boiled shrimp and parsley to the sauce. Stuff peppers and top with cheese, pat of butter and sprinkle of paprika. Bake in 350 degree oven 40 minutes.

Calorie Counter's Vegetable Soup

Slowly boil a 2-pound beef soup bone for 3 to 4 hours. Set aside to cool. Remove the bone and skim all tallow from stock.
Add to stock:

4 stalks celery, diced
3 carrots, diced
1 medium-sized onion, diced
1 cup rutabagas, diced
2 cups raw cabbage, cut up
½ cup peas
½ cup tomatoes
1 tablespoon barley, raw
1 teaspoon salt
4 kernels whole pepper
4 kernels whole allspice
  Enough water for desired consistency

Boil slowly until vegetables are tender. A generous bowl has approximately 100 calories and does fill up a hungry void with health-promoting food, while keeping the calorie count down.

ANOKA COUNTY residents used to flock to the banks of the Rum river early in the spring when the ice went out. It was an exciting time, with the racing waters full of great logs hurried from the Mille Lacs area to the thriving sawmills at Anoka. Fording the river there, too, were the creaking Red River carts full of furs.

Fish Balls

2 pounds boneless raw fish
1 teaspoon melted butter
¼ teaspoon nutmeg
1½ teaspoons salt
¼ teaspoon pepper
1 beaten egg
¼ cup top milk
1 small onion, minced

Force fish through food chopper, using fine blade. Add other ingredients and mix well. Shape into 1½" balls; dip into 1 egg beaten with 3 tablespoons water, then coat with fine bread crumbs. Let stand in refrigerator several hours. Brown slowly on all sides in a little fat.

Wonderful served with new potatoes (boiled in their jackets) and sour cream.

Brazil Nut Treasure Rounds

⅔ cup dates, finely cut
¼ cup Brazil nuts, chopped
¼ cup brown sugar, packed
2 tablespoons water
½ cup shortening (part butter)
¼ pound sharp Cheddar cheese, grated
1 cup plus 2 tablespoons sifted flour

Cook first 4 ingredients until thick; cool. Cream shortening and cheese, blend in flour. Chill 1 hour.

Roll dough ⅛" or less, cut into 2" rounds. Put 1 teaspoon filling on 1 round, cover with another round. To make a pretty cookie, cut a hole in top round with a thimble. Bake at 350 degrees for 15 minutes. Makes 2 dozen.

Chicken Noodle Bake

1 4-pound stewing chicken
4 cups water
1 tablespoon salt
2 onions, sliced
6 whole black peppers
1 clove garlic, minced
1 carrot, halved
Few celery leaves
1 cup celery, sliced
1 cup green pepper, chopped
⅓ cup flour
3 pimientos, chopped
½ teaspoon pepper
1 pound wide noodles
2 cups (½ pound) sharp cheese, shredded
Paprika

Cook first 8 ingredients together slowly, covered, for 3 hours·
Remove meat from chicken; cut in chunks. Strain broth; cool;
skim off fat.

Fry celery and green pepper in chicken fat for 5 minutes. Stir in
flour and add broth plus water to make 3½ cups. Cook until
thickened, stirring constantly. Add pimientos, pepper, and chicken.

Cook noodles as directed on package; drain. Put into 4-quart
casserole; add sauce and mix lightly with fork. Sprinkle with sharp
cheese and paprika. Bake at 375 degrees about 40 minutes or until
bubbly hot. Serves 12. If desired, this can be made and refrigerated
a day ahead; remove 1 hour before time to bake.

Bread-and-Butter Custard Pudding

6 slices stale bread
3 eggs, slightly beaten
½ cup sugar
¼ teaspoon salt
1 quart milk

Spread bread generously with butter. Arrange buttered side
down in casserole or square 8″ x 8″ pan. Slices may be 2 or 3 deep.

Warm milk, add sugar, salt. Add to beaten eggs; pour over bread
slices. Bake 1 hour at 325 degrees. Top will be golden brown.

Walnuts, raisins, or shredded coconut may be added between
bread slices. Serves 6.

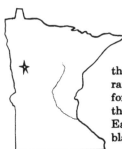

BECKER COUNTY grew up with the logging camps and there's a tale that one million ties for the Northern Pacific railroad tracks came from its forests. What's left of the forests, plus a myriad of lakes, makes the area a leader in the resort industry. Part of the county is in the White Earth reservation, named for the white clay under the black soil.

Old-fashioned Turkey Soup

      3 large onions
      3 stalks celery
      2 medium-sized carrots
      ½ pound butter
   1½ cups flour
      3 quarts turkey (or chicken) stock
      1 pint light cream
        Salt and pepper to taste
      ¼ cup (or more) finely diced cooked turkey
        (or chicken)
      ¼ cup cooked rice

Chop onions, celery, and carrots very fine. Cook with a little water for 20 minutes, or until tender. Melt butter and blend in flour thoroughly. Heat stock and cream and add very gradually to butter and flour mixture, stirring until lumps disappear. Add vegetables, water and all. Stir and cook over low heat for 10 minutes. Season to taste. Add turkey and rice. Yields about 4½ quarts of soup.

To make stock, add 3 quarts water and 1 tablespoon salt to cooked carcass or raw neck and wings. Simmer for several hours. Strain.

Potato Pancakes

The early settlers grew tired of "plain" potatoes. Here's one way they dressed them up.

Peel and grate six large potatoes. Grater must be very fine.

Add:

      1 cup flour
      1 teaspoon sugar
      1 teaspoon salt
      1 teaspoon soda
      ½ cup milk

Stir together well. Fry on a well-greased griddle until brown on both sides. Then place them in a warm oven for a few minutes until they bake through.

Rhubarb Crunch

1 cup sifted flour
¾ cup uncooked oatmeal
1 cup brown sugar
½ cup melted butter
1 teaspoon cinnamon
4 cups rhubarb, diced
1 cup sugar
2 tablespoons cornstarch
1 cup water
1 teaspoon vanilla

Cook white sugar, cornstarch, water until thick; add vanilla. Mix dry ingredients until crumbly, press half into greased 9" pan, cover with rhubarb, then the cooked sauce and balance of crumbs. Bake at 350 degrees for 1 hour. Makes about 12 servings. Serve with whipped cream or ice cream.

Snow Pudding

1 tablespoon gelatin
¼ cup cold water
1 cup boiling water
1 cup sugar
¼ cup lemon juice
3 egg whites, stiffly beaten

Soften gelatin in cold water, dissolve in boiling water. Add sugar and lemon juice. Chill. When mixture thickens, whip and fold in egg whites. Place in mold or molds and chill until firm. Serve with custard sauce.

Custard Sauce

1 cup milk
3 egg yolks
1 teaspoon vanilla
⅛ teaspoon salt
¼ cup sugar

Scald milk, beat egg yolks slightly and stir in sugar and salt. Add egg mixture slowly to scalded milk. Cook over boiling water until mixture coats spoon. This will be very thin and velvety. Remove from heat and stir in vanilla. Chill and serve over snow pudding. Garnish with fresh strawberries rolled in powdered sugar.

BELTRAMI COUNTY is named for an Italian nobleman, tall, strong, proud and hard to get along with. Giacomo C. Beltrami came here in 1823, searching for the source of the Mississippi. He described the area in letters to a lady friend in Italy. Thinking he had found the source in a lake, he named it Julia—in honor of the lady.

Oatmeal Raisin Cookies

½ cup butter
½ cup shortening
1 cup sugar
1 cup raisins
2 eggs
1 teaspoon vanilla
5 tablespoons raisin juice
1 teaspoon soda
2 cups oatmeal
2 cups flour
1 cup nuts, cut fine
¼ teaspoon salt

Cook the raisins in 1 cup of water; boil down so you have 5 tablespoons of raisin juice. Let this cool.

Cream the shortening, sugar; then add eggs and beat well. Mix the dry ingredients together and sift together; add the cool raisin juice, nuts, vanilla, raisins and mix well.

Drop dough by teaspoonfuls on greased cookie sheet and bake about 10 minutes at 375 degrees. Let cool and frost.

Frosting

2 cups sifted powdered sugar
3 tablespoons melted butter
Pinch salt
1 whole egg
1 teaspoon vanilla
Little cream

Beat well and spread on cooled cookies.

Liver Sausage

½ pork liver

1 heart

3 or 4 pounds pork roast or pork trimmings equal that amount

4 or 5 large onions

1 quart flour (about)

½ teaspoon thyme

½ teaspoon cloves

1 teaspoon allspice

Salt to taste

Cook liver in separate pan with enough water to cover until tender. Cook heart and pork in water to cover until well done.

Grind all meat through a food chopper along with onions. Add ground meat and onions to stock from heart and pork. Then add flour and all the spices. Put in ungreased bread pans and bake from 45 minutes to 1 hour at 375 degrees. Cool.

This is very good for a breakfast dish. Slice ½" thick and fry in bacon grease until brown on one side, then turn and brown on other side.

Mushroom Cheese Casserole

1 tablespoon salt

2 cups elbow macaroni

1 small onion

2 tablespoons butter

½ teaspoon dry mustard

1 can cream of mushroom soup

1½ cups milk

¼ pound cheese (more may be used, if desired)

Salt and pepper to your taste

4 graham crackers

Cook macaroni in salted, boiling water for about 9 minutes or until tender.

While macaroni is cooking, mince onion fine. Put in a sauce pan with butter, dry mustard, mushroom soup, milk, and cheese. Heat on low flame, stirring occasionally, until cheese is melted and sauce is creamy.

When macaroni is cooked, drain and turn into a buttered casserole dish. Pour sauce over macaroni, salt and pepper according to your taste, then toss lightly with a fork so all macaroni gets nicely covered.

Top with strips of cheese and sprinkle with graham cracker crumbs. Bake uncovered about 25 minutes at 375 degrees. Chopped green pepper may be added. Also, if more mushrooms are desired, a small can of button mushrooms may be added.

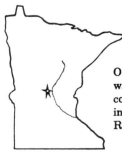

BENTON COUNTY has a town once known as Peep O'Day. There the Foley brothers built a sawmill which was the origin of Foley, now the county seat. Benton county, in 1886, suffered an historic tornado. It killed 75 in Sauk Rapids, then swept through a wedding party near Rice, killing the groom, the minister and nine guests.

Poppy Seed Bread

This is a family tradition. My parents and grandparents raised their own poppy seed, but today we can buy it, of course. This bread was always served on special occasions such as the Christmas holidays and Easter. Mrs. Louis Bolinski, Sauk Rapids.

4 cups sifted flour
½ cup sugar
1½ teaspoons salt
¼ teaspoon ground cardamom
2 eggs
1 cup milk
1 cake yeast
2 tablespoons shortening

Dissolve yeast in lukewarm water. Knead in same manner as bread, and let rise until double in bulk.

Roll about ¼" thick, spread filling as thick as you wish, roll into loaf, and let rise 1 hour. Brush top with shortening. Bake at 350 degrees about 40 minutes. Makes 2 loaves.

Filling

2 cups poppy seed
2 cups sugar
4 whole eggs
½ teaspoon cinnamon

Soak poppy seed in cold water overnight. In morning, drain in fine strainer until all water is drained. Grind in meat grinder, using finest cutter. Add sugar, eggs, and cinnamon. Mix thoroughly.

Pork Sausage Dressing

1 pound pork sausage
½ loaf bread
4 eggs
Salt and pepper
½ cup flour
4 small onions

Mix well. Use in either chicken or turkey, also veal pockets.

Cherry Delight

1 can cherries
1 cup water
1 cup sugar
3 tablespoons cornstarch
¼ cup water
40 marshmallows
1¼ cups milk
1¼ cups whipping cream
1⅓ cups graham cracker crumbs
⅓ cup butter, melted
3 tablespoons sugar

Simmer cherries, water, and sugar for 5 minutes, then thicken with cornstarch and water. Cool. Dissolve marshmallows in milk in double boiler. Cool. Whip cream and add to cooled marshmallow mixture. Mix melted butter, sugar, graham crumbs, and pat into bottom of pan, reserving some crumbs for topping. Put pan in refrigerator to set crumbs.

Pour half the marshmallow mixture over the crumbs. Spoon the cherry mixture over this. Add rest of marshmallow mixture. Top with crumbs. Serve with whipping cream topped off with a cherry.

Christmas Cruller (Swedish Klenater)

4 egg yolks
¼ cup powdered sugar
3 tablespoons butter
1½ cups flour
1 tablespoon brandy
1 tablespoon lemon rind, grated

Mix ingredients and stir until well blended. Chill. Turn dough onto floured baking board. Roll out thin. With pastry wheel, cut strips ¾" wide and 3" long. Cut gash in center and twist one end through it. Fry in deep fat, 375 degrees, until light brown. Drain on absorbent paper. Makes 50.

Sour Cream Dressing (Polish)

3 hard-boiled eggs
1 cup sour cream
1½ to 2 teaspoons lemon juice or vinegar
Sugar, salt, paprika

Mash the yolks of 2 hard-cooked eggs and add the sugar, sour cream, and lemon juice or vinegar to taste. Mix well. Pour over the prepared lettuce and garnish with the remaining hard-cooked egg. Sprinkle with salt and paprika.

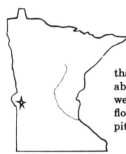

BIG STONE COUNTY borrowed the name of the lake that bounds it on the west. Great granite boulders lie about the lake. And the claim shanties of the early settlers were put up near the water. One settler, writing of dirt floors and beds of hay, said, "We make up the beds with a pitchfork and sweep the floor with a shingle."

Real Norwegian Lefsa

> 4 cups white flour
> 3 cups graham flour
> ¼ cup lard
> 1 teaspoon salt

Add milk enough to make a dough stiffer than bread dough. Work all together well. Form into 2½" long rolls and cut into 1" slices. Roll out as thin as possible and bake on top of hot stove or on lefsa grill. Then lay on table in between towels until it has all been baked on 1 side only.

For the topping to make them white, mix 3 cups skimmed milk and ½ pound cornstarch together. Put 2 tablespoons or more of this on the unbaked side of each lefsa and rub it in with the palm of the hand until it looks smooth. Again bake on top of stove or grill until the cornstarch is dry and white.

Store flat on towels, with a weight on top.

To serve, pour boiling water on baked side, let stand a few minutes covered. Spread with butter, sugar, and cinnamon or butter, sugar, and primost. Fold and cut into pieces.

Jiffy Biscuits

> 2 cups flour
> 2 teaspoons baking powder
> 1 teaspoon salt
> 1 tablespoon sugar
> 1¼ cups heavy cream

Sift flour, baking powder, salt, and sugar together well; stir in cream just until mixture sticks together. It will seem rather dry. Drop (or roll and cut) on greased pan and bake 12 minutes at 400 degrees.

Fruit Soup (Danish Sodsuppe)

This attractive fruit soup is easily varied and may be served as a dessert with a scoop of whipped cream topping.

    8 cups boiling water (or part juice
        from cherry or plum sauce)
    1 cup sugar
    ½ teaspoon salt
    ½ cup tapioca
    1 cup prunes
    ½ cup raisins or currants
    ½ orange, cut into small pieces
    ½ lemon, cut into small pieces
    3 apples, pared and diced
    3 peaches, pared and diced
    2 sticks cinnamon

Boil water, sugar, and salt; gradually add tapioca and remaining ingredients. Simmer slowly about 1 hour. To shorten the cooking time, soak the tapioca in ½ cup cold water 15 minutes before adding it to the liquid. Serve the soup hot or cold with croutons or buttered rye bread.

Rum Pudding (Danish)

    3 egg yolks
    6 tablespoons sugar
    ¼ teaspoon salt
    2 tablespoons rum (½ tablespoon vanilla
        or 1 teaspoon almond extract may be
        substituted)
    1 tablespoon gelatin, unflavored
    ¾ cup cold water
    1 cup whipped cream

Beat yolks, sugar, and salt well; add rum. Soak gelatin in cold water, stirring over hot water until gelatin is dissolved; add to egg mixture. When it begins to thicken, fold in whipped cream. Chill and serve with warm fruit sauce.

    Fruit Sauce
    1 cup sweetened fruit juice
        (raspberry, cherry, or plum)
    2 tablespoons potato flour or cornstarch

Cook until slightly thickened.

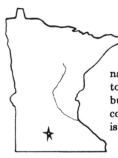

BLUE EARTH COUNTY and the river, too, earned their name from the clay the Indians dug from the river banks to decorate their faces. When Pierre Charles LeSueur built Fort L'Huillier in 1700, he thought the clay was copper ore, and shipped two tons of it to France. Mankato is the white man's attempt to spell the Sioux "blue earth."

Graham-Molasses-Raisin Bread

My grandmother called this bread Brown Bread. She used old-fashioned bran flour, black strap molasses, saleratus, and buttermilk. Through the years I have varied the flours, even to adding pulverized box cereal, and wheat germ, but keeping amounts in balance. I like cut-up maraschinos, grated orange rind or nuts added, too. Mary Salinda Foster, Mankato.

3 cups graham flour
1 cup white flour
2½ cups sweet or sour milk
⅔ cup molasses
⅓ cup sugar
1 teaspoon salt
2 teaspoons soda
2 cups raisins

Blend milk, molasses, sugar, salt, and soda. Add graham flour, white flour, then raisins. Pour mixture into two greased loaf pans. Let stand 45 minutes before baking. Bake in moderate oven (350 degrees) for 1 hour.

Washington Cherry-ettes

¾ cup shortening
½ cup powdered sugar
1 teaspoon salt
2 teaspoons vanilla
2 cups sifted all-purpose flour
1 cup chopped pecans
20 candied cherries

Blend together shortening, salt, sugar, and vanilla. Add flour and pecans and mix into a soft dough. Measure out level tablespoonfuls of dough and roll between palms of hands to form round balls. Place on greased baking sheets. Press a hole in center of each ball and insert half a cherry. Bake in slow oven (325 degrees) for 25 minutes. The recipe makes about 3 dozen cookies.

Baked Turkey Salad

3 cups cooked turkey or chicken, diced
3 cups celery, diced
1 cup walnuts, chopped
4 teaspoons onion, minced
1 teaspoon salt
⅛ teaspoon pepper
1½ cups mayonnaise
¼ cup lemon juice
2 cups potato chips, crushed

Toss all together lightly and heap into 8 individual baking dishes or in two 9″ pans. Sprinkle tops with crushed potato chips, bake at 450 degrees for 15 minutes or until lightly browned. Serves 8.

Twenty Minute Eggs a la King

1 can condensed mushroom soup
¼ cup milk
½ cup sharp Cheddar cheese, cut up
4 hard-boiled eggs, sliced
¼ cup chopped pimiento
Toast

Heat the soup, milk, and cheese over low heat, stirring well until cheese is melted. Add eggs and pimiento and serve on toast. One teaspoon of Worcestershire sauce may be added to the sauce mixture before mixing in the eggs.

Circle Eight Corn Bread

¾ cup yellow corn meal
1¼ cups enriched sifted flour
¼ cup sugar
½ teaspoon baking powder
1 slightly beaten egg
¾ cup milk
¼ cup bacon fryings
8 slices bacon, fried until crisp and
   broken into bits

Sift dry ingredients into a bowl and make a well in center. Add egg and milk, stirring lightly, fold in melted fat and bacon bits. Bake in a round mold or tubular cake tin at 425 degrees for 30 minutes. Serve while warm.

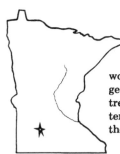

BROWN COUNTY'S settlers, many of them German workingmen from the cathedral town of Ulm, were just getting a toehold when the Sioux, bitter over recent treaties, invaded it in 1862 and massacred 200 in two terrible days. Imitation cannon made of stovepipe, and the beating of anvils finally helped drive the Indians away.

Peach Angel Meringue

    5 egg whites
    ½ teaspoon salt
    1 cup sugar
    6 to 8 peach halves, drained
    Whipped cream
    Maraschino cherries, chopped
    California walnuts, broken

Preheat oven to 450 degrees. Beat egg whites with salt until soft peaks are formed. Gradually beat in sugar. Continue to beat until stiff peaks are formed, about 15 minutes. Spread mixture in well-greased 8" x 8" x 2" pan. Place in preheated oven and close door. Turn off heat and let meringue stand overnight or for 5 hours before removing from oven.

To serve, cut meringue in squares. Place a peach half, cut side up, on top of each serving. Fill center with whipped cream, cherry slices and nuts. Makes 6 to 8 servings. This is excellent with fresh strawberries and raspberries also.

Cauliflower Superb

    1 medium-sized head cauliflower
    1 8-ounce can mushrooms, drained
    ¼ cup green pepper, diced
    ⅓ cup butter
    ¼ cup flour
    2 cups milk
    1 teaspoon salt
    6 ounces pimiento cheese

Brown mushrooms and green pepper in butter. Add flour, then stir in milk and cook until thick, stirring constantly. Meanwhile cook cauliflower, which has been broken into small pieces, about 10 minutes.

Place half of cauliflower into bottom of 1½-quart casserole, then add half of sauce, then half of cheese. Repeat. Bake in 350 degree oven for 15 minutes. Serve immediately.

27

Swedish Potato Sausage (Potatis Korv)

2½ pounds pork butt, ground
½ pound ground beef
6 raw potatoes
1 cup milk, scalded
1 medium-sized onion
1 teaspoon pepper
2 to 3 tablespoons salt
¾ teaspoon allspice
2 teaspoons ginger
1 pound casings

Grind potatoes and onions and mix with the ground meat. Add spices, salt, and milk and mix thoroughly. Cut casing in 24" lengths; tie one end of casing and fill with sausage mixture; allow space for expansion so casings do not break during cooking. Tie other end. Prick in several places before cooking. Boil slowly 45 minutes.

Heavenly Delight Hot Dish

1 pound veal steak, cubed
1 pound pork steak, cubed
Onion to taste
1½ pounds American cheese, cubed
1 No. 2 can whole kernel corn
½ pound raw noodles
2 cans chicken rice soup
1 green pepper, chopped
1 4-ounce can pimiento, chopped
1 8-ounce can mushrooms
Browned and buttered bread crumbs

Brown meat with a little onion. Combine ingredients in casserole and top with buttered bread crumbs. Bake at 300 degrees for 1 hour.

South Sea Ribs

2 sides of pork spareribs
1 cup soy sauce
½ cup sugar
1 teaspoon salt
2 tablespoons catsup

Trim ribs of all fat and skin. Separate each rib. Marinate ribs in mixture 1 hour (no more). Roast at 400 degrees for 30 minutes; baste frequently.

CARLTON COUNTY'S seat is Carlton. It was there, in 1870, that two men filled a wheelbarrow with dirt and trundled it off to dump it on the site of a proposed railroad grade. It was a ceremony marking the start of the Northern Pacific. Later the first spike was driven and crews started laying steel.

Peanut Butter Pinwheels

½ cup shortening
1 cup sugar
½ cup chunk style peanut butter
1 egg
2 tablespoons milk
1¼ cups flour
½ teaspoon salt
½ teaspoon soda
1 6-ounce package chocolate chips
1 teaspoon butter

Cream shortening and sugar; add peanut butter, egg, and milk. Sift dry ingredients and add to first mixture. Divide into 2 parts and roll each into a rectangle. Melt chocolate over hot water, add butter. Spread over the rolled dough and roll up like a jelly roll. Chill about 30 minutes before slicing. Bake at 375 degrees for 8 to 10 minutes.

Confetti Dip for Chips

3 eggs, beaten well
3 tablespoons sugar
3 tablespoons vinegar
1 tablespoon butter
½ pound cream cheese
Few drops Tabasco sauce
1 small onion, chopped
1 sweet red pepper, chopped
1 green pepper, chopped
Season to taste

Combine beaten eggs, sugar, vinegar. Cook over hot water until mixture thickens. Stir constantly. Add butter and cream cheese. Beat until smooth. Add Tabasco and chopped onion and peppers.

Applesauce Cake

1½ cups white sugar
1 cup brown sugar
¾ cup shortening (part butter)
2 large eggs
1 teaspoon cloves
½ teaspoon allspice
2 teaspoons cinnamon
½ teaspoon nutmeg
1 teaspoon lemon extract
½ cup molasses

Mix the above well. Then add:

2½ cups mashed applesauce
½ cup raisins
2 teaspoons soda
3½ cups flour

Sprinkle top with crushed nuts and sugar. No other frosting required. Bake in slow oven, about 325 degrees, 1 hour.

Pancakes with Cranberry Sauce (Finnish)

1 cup sifted flour
1½ cups milk
2 eggs, separated
¼ cup sugar
½ teaspoon salt
¼ teaspoon cinnamon
1 tablespoon melted butter
Sliced apple

Mix flour and milk until smooth. Add beaten egg yolks, then sugar, salt, cinnamon, and butter. Mix well and add beaten egg whites.

Form small pancakes on greased pancake griddle or frying pan. Use 1 or 2 slices of apple on each cake. Bake like any pancake and serve with Cranberry Sauce.

Cranberry Sauce
4 cups fresh cranberries
1 cup water
2½ cups sugar
½ lemon, sliced thin

Boil all together until slightly thickened. Stir to prevent scorching. Serve on pancakes.

CARVER COUNTY'S story is the tale of the frontier. Its settlers came from northern Europe; they were carpenters, masons, shoemakers, tanners, blacksmiths. Though they couldn't always speak each other's tongue, they could trade talents to clear the "Big Woods," build cabins, and start the farms of this important dairy area.

Pea Timbals

2 onions, cut in large chunks
2 tablespoons butter
1 teaspoon garlic salt
1 teaspoon paprika
½ teaspoon salt
¼ teaspoon pepper
4 eggs, beaten
2 tablespoons heavy cream
(or evaporated milk)
2 cups cooked peas (canned or frozen)

Sauté onions to light brown in butter to which all seasonings have been added. Beat the eggs with cream and add to first mixture. Add cooked peas and pour into greased baking dish. Stir before baking. Place dish in pan of hot water and bake at 350 degrees for 1 hour or until silver knife comes out clean.

This can be prepared a day ahead and put in refrigerator until ready to bake.

Meat Ball Chop Suey

1 cup boiling water
½ cup raw rice
1 egg, beaten
1 pound ground beef
Salt and pepper to taste
¾ cup onion, chopped
1½ cups celery, diced
1 can cream of celery soup
3 tablespoons soy sauce

Pour boiling water over rice in a 2-quart casserole and let stand while preparing remaining ingredients. Mix egg with ground beef, salt, pepper, and ¼ of the chopped onion. Form into 1½″ balls, brown in small amount of fat. Add with the remaining ingredients, including onion, to rice. Cover and bake at 350 degrees for 75 minutes.

Snow Balls

½ cup butter
1 pound dates
½ cup sugar
1 egg, well beaten
¼ cup milk
1 teaspoon vanilla
2 cups Rice Krispies
½ cup nuts, finely chopped
Shredded coconut

Cook butter, dates, and sugar together slowly until dates are soft. Remove from heat and add well-beaten egg and the milk. Cool this mixture and then add remaining ingredients, except coconut. Butter your hands; roll dough into balls and then roll the balls in shredded coconut. Keep in refrigerator or freezer.

Curried Rice and Chicken

1 cup rice
1 onion
1 teaspoon curry powder
2 teaspoons salt
2 cups cooked chicken, diced
3 cups chicken broth
2 tablespoons butter

Cover rice with cold water, bring quickly to boiling point, then drain and rinse in cold water. Now cook the rice in chicken broth until almost done.

Mix the curry powder in 1 tablespoon butter and add to rice. Sauté the finely-chopped onion in remaining 1 tablespoon butter and add to rice. Bake at 300 degrees until almost ready to serve. Add the chicken and serve.

Quantity Hot Dish

2 pounds medium noodles
2 cups onions, chopped
2 quarts celery, diced
2 No. 2½ cans mushrooms
5 pounds ground beef
1 cup molasses
1 quart tomato purée, juice, or soup
1½ quarts tomatoes
7 tablespoons salt

Brown onions, celery, and mushrooms in a little fat; add meat and brown lightly. Cook the noodles. Mix all together and bake at 350 degrees until done. Serves 50.

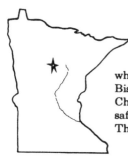

CASS COUNTY and Cass lake are named for an explorer who thought the lake was the source of the Mississippi. Bishop Whipple, pioneer Episcopalian, once started a Chippewa mission at the lake. Asking a chief if it were safe to leave his valise, the bishop was told, "Oh yes. There is no other white man in this part of the country."

Shrimp and Wild Rice

1 tablespoon finely-chopped onion
1 cup whole shrimp
1 cup cream
1 tablespoon butter
1 cup cooked wild rice
2 tablespoons catsup

Brown the finely-chopped onion in butter. Add shrimp, wild rice, and cream. Let simmer for 20 minutes. Add the catsup; let simmer for 10 minutes. Serve in mound, sprinkled liberally with paprika and a few chopped scallions.

Chicken Loaf

2 cups cooked chicken
2 cups soft bread crumbs
1 cup diced, cooked carrots
1 cup cooked green peas
1 medium-sized onion
1 tablespoon shortening
2 eggs
1 teaspoon sage
Salt
Pepper

To the bread crumbs add peas, carrots, onion (browned in the shortening), and seasonings; add egg yolks, beaten. Mix thoroughly but lightly, then add chicken and lastly add the 2 egg whites beaten stiff. Fold into mixture carefully. Grease a shallow pan generously and put in mixture. Bake about 1½ hours in 350 degree oven. Make a medium thick gravy of chicken broth and serve hot with the chicken loaf.

33

Blueberry Nut Bread

2 eggs
1 cup sugar
1 cup milk
3 tablespoons shortening, melted
3 cups flour
1 teaspoon salt
4 teaspoons baking powder
½ cup nuts
1 cup fresh blueberries

Beat eggs, add sugar gradually. Add milk and melted shortening. Sift flour, salt, baking powder and add to liquid. Stir only enough to blend. Fold in nuts and blueberries.

Pour into well-greased 5″ x 12″ loaf pan or two 3½″ x 7½″ Pyrex loaf pans. Bake in 350 degree oven for 1 hour or until done.

Ozark Pudding

1 egg
¾ cup sugar
2 tablespoons flour
1¼ teaspoons baking powder
⅛ teaspoon salt
½ cup chopped nuts
½ cup chopped apple
1 teaspoon vanilla

Beat eggs and sugar together until very smooth. Mix flour, baking powder, and salt. Add to egg mixture. Add nuts, apple, and vanilla. Bake in greased pie tin in 350 degree oven for 35 or 40 minutes. Serve with whipped cream.

Carrot Mold

2 cups of cooked, mashed carrots
2 eggs, beaten
½ teaspoon salt
¼ teaspoon pepper
2 tablespoons sugar
¼ cup cream

Mix in order given. Place in a well-greased ring mold. Place mold in a pan of hot water. Bake at 350 degrees until set. Test as for pumpkin pie. Unmold and serve creamed vegetables in the center.

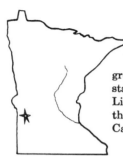

CHIPPEWA COUNTY'S first known white settler was a gruff, stubborn Scot, Murdock Cameron who, in 1800, started a trading post near Lac qui Parle lake. When Lieutenant Zebulon Pike came to the state in 1805 to force the English to give up the area, he took time to reprimand Cameron for selling firewater to the Indians.

Wild Rice Casserole

Soak 1½ cups wild rice overnight, then pour off water several times and start cooking and pouring water off until the water is clear. Then add water again, this time salted and cook until tender, drain and add:

> ¼ **pound bacon, chopped**
> 1 **medium-sized onion, chopped**
> 1 **stalk celery, chopped**
> **Mushrooms, to your liking**

First fry bacon until almost brown, then add onion, celery, and mushrooms and cook together for about 5 or 10 minutes and add to drained rice. Bake in casserole for about half hour, or until well blended and cooked together. Also add salt, pepper, and a little spice if you like it.

Sunny Silver Torte

> **Crust**
> 1½ **cups flour**
> ¾ **cup butter**

Sift flour, cut in butter until like fine crumbs. Press into 9"x13" pan. Bake in moderate oven (350 degrees) for 30 minutes.

> **Custard**
> 8 **eggs, separated**
> 1 **cup sugar**
> **Juice of 2 lemons and 1 orange**
> **Rind of 1 lemon and 1 orange**
> 1½ **tablespoons gelatin**
> ¾ **cup cold water**
> ½ **cup sugar (for egg whites)**

Dissolve gelatin in water, let stand. Beat egg yolks in top of double boiler, add sugar, juice, and rinds. Cook until creamy. Add gelatin, mix and let set awhile.

Beat egg whites until stiff, add ½ cup sugar and fold into the slightly cooled custard. Pour over crust and let stand overnight. Cut into squares and serve with whipped cream.

"Spek'n Dek'n" (German pancake dish)

        3 eggs
        1 teaspoon salt
        2 cups heavy syrup
        ½ cup sugar
        1½ quarts sour milk, plus 1 teaspoon soda
        2 cups white flour
        3½ cups rye meal
        3 teaspoons caraway seed
        1 metwurst, sliced into batter
        1 metwurst, sliced and fried slowly

Beat the eggs, salt, syrup, and sugar together. Add milk, blend in flour, rye meal, and caraway seed. Add 1 sliced metwurst to batter; begin frying other sliced metwurst. Drop batter by spoonfuls over the sliced metwurst on the grill. Continue frying until brown. Serve with butter and syrup.

White Fruit Cake

        1 cup butter
        2 cups sugar
        3 cups flour
        1½ teaspoons baking powder
        1 cup milk
        ½ pound white raisins
        1 cup almonds (⅓ pound)
        1 cup candied cherries (½ pound)
        4 slices candied pineapple (red and green)
        2 cups coconut, ground
        5 egg whites, beaten stiff and folded in last

Line gold-lined vegetable cans with waxed paper and fill half full. Put on cookie sheet and bake 1 hour or more at 300 degrees.

Mother's Graham Gems

        1 cup graham flour
        1 cup white flour, plus 1 teaspoon soda
        1 teaspoon salt
        2 tablespoons molasses or brown sugar
        3 tablespoons melted butter
        1 egg
        1 cup sour milk or buttermilk

Mix dry ingredients, add milk, beaten egg, molasses, and shortening. Bake in greased gem pans at 400 degrees for 25 minutes.

CHISAGO COUNTY adjoins the St. Croix river, a highway for the voyageurs 250 years ago, and later for great lumber drives. Then came the Swedish settlers, encouraged by Eric Norelius, long-time Lutheran leader who would conduct morning services at Chisago Lake, then walk 10 miles to Taylors Falls for afternoon prayers.

Cherry Roll-ups

2 cups flour
4 teaspoons baking powder
2 tablespoons sugar
½ teaspoon salt
¼ cup shortening
⅔ cup milk
1 can cherries
1 cup sugar
½ cup water
¼ cup sugar

Cut shortening into flour, baking powder, sugar, and salt. Add milk; roll dough out to ¼" thickness and brush with melted butter. Spread drained cherries and 1 cup of sugar over dough and then roll up like jelly roll. Slice into ¾" slices and put cut-side down on cookie sheet. Brush each slice generously with mixture of ¼ cup sugar and ½ cup water that has been boiled for 10 minutes. Bake at 425 degrees for 10 minutes; reduce heat to 350 and bake 10 minutes longer. Serve with hot cherry sauce.

Cherry Sauce

½ cup cherry juice
½ cup water
½ cup sugar
1 teaspoon butter
½ teaspoon almond extract
1 tablespoon cornstarch (or more)

Boil all ingredients together until sauce is of desired thickness.

Chantilly Potatoes

Mash boiled or baked potatoes, add salt and pepper but not quite as much cream as for regular mashed potatoes. Put in casserole; place in oven to keep hot.

Beat ½ pint cream, add a dash of salt, and fold in 1 tablespoon of Parmesan cheese. Pile whipped cream on top of potatoes and bake at 425 degrees for 10 minutes. Serve immediately.

Beef Chunks in Sour Cream

> 3 pounds lean stewing beef,
> cut into 1" cubes
>
> 3 tablespoons fat
>
> 2 medium-sized onions, sliced thin
>
> 1½ cups sour cream
>
> 1 cup mushrooms, sliced
>
> ½ teaspoon oregano
>
> ¼ teaspoon sweet basil
>
> 1 teaspoon salt
>
> 1½ teaspoons paprika

Roll beef cubes in flour, brown in fat. Add onions and brown. Add sour cream, mushrooms, and spices. Cover and simmer over low heat about 1¾ hours, or until meat is tender. Stir occasionally during cooking. Makes 6 to 8 servings.

Peach Praline Pie

> Pastry for one 9" pie shell
>
> 4 cups (about 3 pounds) sliced,
> peeled ripe peaches
>
> ½ cup granulated sugar
>
> 2 tablespoons quick-cooking tapioca
>
> 1 teaspoon lemon juice
>
> ½ cup sifted flour
>
> ¼ cup brown sugar, firmly packed
>
> ½ cup pecans, chopped
>
> ¼ cup butter

Combine peaches, granulated sugar, tapioca, and lemon juice in large bowl; let stand 15 minutes.

Combine flour, brown sugar, and pecans in small bowl; cut in butter with fork or mix with fingertips until crumbly. Sprinkle 1/3 of pecan mixture over bottom of pie shell; cover with peach mixture; sprinkle remaining pecan mixture over peaches.

Bake pie at 450 degrees for 10 minutes; reduce heat to 350 degrees and bake 20 minutes longer, or until peaches are tender and topping golden brown.

CLAY COUNTY'S story lies around the Red river on its west. That river may have brought the Vikings here before Columbus. Traders used it to come from Hudson Bay to a post at Georgetown. Red River carts loaded with furs for Mendota followed a trail along its banks and dog sled toboggans used the trail in winter.

Ham and Potato Chowder

¼ cup melted butter
1 medium-sized onion, minced
¾ cup baked or boiled ham, diced
½ cup celery, chopped
1½ cups raw potatoes, finely diced
3 tablespoons flour
2 cups milk
1½ teaspoons salt
¼ teaspoon pepper

Saute'the chopped onion, ham, and chopped celery in the melted butter. Add the diced potatoes and cook for 10 minutes longer. Remove from the heat and add the salt, pepper, flour, and milk. Mix well. Return to heat and warm slowly. Do not let the soup boil. More milk may be added to thin the soup to desired consistency. Makes 4 to 6 servings.

Steak Louisiana

1½ pounds round steak, 1" thick
Flour with salt and pepper added
3 tablespoons fat
2 medium-sized onions, thinly sliced
1 No. 303 can tomatoes
1 cup tomato juice
1 tablespoon Parmesan cheese, grated
1 green pepper, cut into rings
4 medium-sized yams, peeled and
sliced ¾" thick
Salt and pepper to taste

Dredge meat in seasoned flour. Melt fat over low heat; add onion slices and cook until golden brown. Remove. Brown meat well on both sides. Add tomatoes, tomato juice, cheese, and green pepper rings. Top with onion rings. Cover; cook over low heat until meat is tender (about 1 hour). Add yam slices. Cover; continue cooking until yams are tender, about 15 minutes. Season to taste with salt and pepper. Makes 4 to 6 servings.

Seafood-stuffed Potatoes

4 large baking potatoes
½ cup butter
½ cup rich milk or cream
1 6½-ounce can crabmeat, lobster, or tuna
1 teaspoon salt
⅛ teaspoon cayenne pepper
2 tablespoons onion, grated
1 cup sharp Cheddar cheese, grated
½ teaspoon paprika

Bake potatoes until done. Cut lengthwise slice off each potato near the top. Scoop out potato pulp and whip. Add cream and butter and whip until fluffy. Add rest of ingredients and mix thoroughly. Refill potato shells and place in 450 degree oven for 15 minutes. Serve with another fresh vegetable and tossed green salad. Makes 4 servings.

Cranberry Crisp Mold

1 package lemon Jello
1 cup boiling water
½ cup cold water
1 unpeeled orange
2 cups raw cranberries
1 cup sugar
1 tablespoon lemon juice

Dissolve Jello in boiling water, add cold water and chill until syrupy. Cut orange into 6 wedges; remove seeds. Put orange and cranberries through food chopper, using coarse knife; blend in sugar and lemon juice. Let stand a few minutes to dissolve sugar. Stir fruit mixture into syrupy gelatin; spoon into 1-quart mold; chill until firm. Unmold and serve with your favorite salad dressing.

Konge Cake (King's cake)

23 graham crackers
½ cup sugar
½ cup butter
1 cup milk
1 teaspoon baking powder
1 teaspoon vanilla

Crush crackers, add baking powder, then butter, sugar, milk, and vanilla. Bake in two round layer tins in moderate oven (350 degrees). Put either pineapple or lemon filling between the layers and whipped cream on top. Apricot jam also makes a good filling.

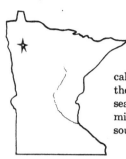

CLEARWATER COUNTY encloses a lake the Indians called Omushkos and the French called *La Biche*. It was the object of one of history's great treasure hunts, the search for the source of the Mississippi river. Finally a mineralogist named Henry R. Schoolcraft determined the source was Omushkos and renamed it Lake Itasca.

Surprise Chocolate Dessert

2 6-ounce packages chocolate bits
2 tablespoons sugar
3 egg yolks, well beaten
3 egg whites, beaten stiff
2 cups heavy cream, whipped
1 angel food cake

Melt chocolate in double boiler, add sugar and egg yolks. Mix thoroughly. Remove from heat and fold in whipped cream and egg whites. Tear angel cake into bite-sized pieces. Put layer in buttered pan about 8" x 12" x 2", using half of cake—cover with layer of chocolate mixture and repeat. Place in refrigerator overnight. Cut in squares. Serves 16.

Coconut Tempters

2 cups sugar
½ cup cocoa
½ cup milk
½ cup butter
½ cup crunchy peanut butter
1 teaspoon vanilla
3 cups quick-cooking oatmeal
¼ cup coconut
1 cup walnuts

Place sugar, cocoa, milk, butter in sauce pan, cook to boiling, stirring constantly. Boil 1 minute, add peanut butter and vanilla and stir until dissolved. Pour over oatmeal and coconut mixture. Mix thoroughly and beat until mixture begins to thicken. Drop from a teaspoon on waxed paper and cool.

Baked Vegetable Dish

> 1 cup uncooked rice
> 1 cup diced onions
> 1 cup diced carrots, raw
> 1 cup diced potatoes, raw
> 1 cup peas (save liquid for adding to
> the baked dish, as it bakes)
> 1 cup tomatoes
> Pork links

Season and bake for 45 minutes or until done. Take from oven and line top with pork links, place in oven and bake until links are brown.

Chocolate Syrup Dessert

> ¼ cup butter
> 1 cup powdered sugar
> 3 egg yolks, beaten
> 24 marshmallows, cut fine
> 1 small can chocolate syrup
> 1 cup chopped pecans
> 3 egg whites, beaten stiff
> 1½ cups graham cracker or
> vanilla wafer crumbs

Mix butter, sugar, yolks, marshmallows, syrup, and pecans. Fold in egg whites. Place half of crumbs in bottom of pan. Pour in chocolate mixture and put remainder of crumbs on top. Chill 12 hours. Serve with whipped cream.

Meat Balls (Swedish Kottbullar)

> 3 pounds hamburger
> 1 egg
> 1½ cups rich milk or cream
> ½ teaspoon pepper
> ½ teaspoon allspice
> 1 cup bread crumbs
> 1 tablespoon flour
> 1 tablespoon cornstarch
> 1 onion
> Salt
> 1 teaspoon sugar

Chop onion and fry until brown. Add to the other ingredients and form into small balls and fry.

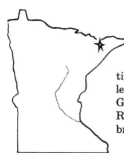

COOK COUNTY with its wonderful wilderness, is that tip of the state north of Lake Superior where the voyageurs left the water and carried their canoes across the nine-mile Grand Portage to the Pigeon River. Even before the Revolution, Grand Portage was a busy settlement, with brisk trade, French fashions, saloons and even police.

Moose or Deer Mince Meat

4 pounds beef, moose, or deer
9 pounds apples
2 pounds suet
3 pounds raisins
2 pounds currants
½ pound citron
1 quart sherry ⎱ or grape juice
½ pint brandy ⎰
5 pounds brown sugar
3 teaspoons cloves
10 teaspoons cinnamon
6 tablespoons salt
1 quart cider and vinegar, mixed
1 quart molasses
2 lemons, juice and rind

Cook until done, and can.

Chocolate Potato Cake

2 cups sugar
1 cup fat
1 cup mashed potato
3 eggs
3 cups flour
1 teaspoon vanilla
½ cup nuts
¼ cup cocoa
1 cup sweet milk
2 teaspoons baking powder
½ cup raisins

Cream sugar and fat, add potatoes and cocoa, mix thoroughly. Add beaten eggs and beat until mixture is smooth. Add dry ingredients (sifted together) and the milk, alternately, reserving a little flour to dredge the nuts and raisins. Add vanilla. Bake 1 hour in 350 degree oven. Makes 1 large loaf or 2 large layers.

Potato Soup

For 4 hungry people, take 4 large potatoes, pared and cubed, and boil these in 3 cups water, seasoned with salt, pepper (or peppercorns), 1 large bay leaf, and 1 medium-sized onion, cut fine. When potatoes are tender, break up some of the cubes with a fork, add 1 cup milk or ⅓ cup cream, and a little butter.

Crisp 8 or more slices of bacon, broken into small pieces, and put into each serving of soup. Top with finely-cut parsley.

Baked Pheasant Deluxe

        2 birds, cut to serve
        ½ cup flour
        2 teaspoons salt
        ¼ teaspoon pepper
        ½ cup butter
        2 tablespoons onion juice
        ¼ cup chopped parsley
        2 cups sour cream

Have meat washed well, and dry. Dredge it in flour, salt, pepper. Brown meat slowly in butter. Place in baking dish. Add onion juice and parsley to the cream, mix well and pour over browned meat.

Cover and bake at 325 degrees until tender, from 1½ to 2½ hours.

Serves 6 or 8 people.

Roast Wild Duck or Goose

        2 wild fowl, ready to roast
        1½ teaspoons salt
        ⅓ cup butter
        1 cup onions, chopped
        1 cup diced celery
        2 cups diced apples
        4 cups drained kraut
        Giblets, chopped

Melt butter, add chopped giblets, onion, and celery and cook 20 minutes, slowly. Blend in apple and kraut.

Fill fowl with this stuffing. Truss up fowl and place in roaster. Cover, bake at 325 degrees slowly for 3 hours. Baste often with pan drippings and liquid drained from kraut.

Uncover last half hour to brown. Lay a couple slices of fresh pork over fowl while baking.

COTTONWOOD COUNTY was vast prairie when the settlers came. They couldn't build log cabins so their first homes were of mud. They burrowed into a hillside, for warmth; made walls of mud-daubed stakes. Bright green grass often sprouted from the sod roofs. Prairie fires, bitter blizzards and Indian raids added no comfort to a hard life.

Kentist Cake (English)

½ cup butter
¾ cup sugar
2 eggs
2 tablespoons coconut
2 tablespoons cocoa
1 teaspoon vanilla
½ cup milk
1 cup flour
1 teaspoon baking powder
½ cup chopped nuts
¼ cup cherries
½ cup raisins

Bake for about 1 hour in 325 degree oven in loaf bread pan. Frost with chocolate frosting and sprinkle with chopped nuts.

Zwieback

1 cake yeast
½ cup lukewarm water
1 teaspoon sugar
3 cups flour
¾ cups shortening (half lard, hε'f butter)
3½ teaspoons salt
2 cups scalded milk

Dissolve yeast in lukewarm water. Add sugar. Sift flour into a bowl, add shortening, salt, scalded milk, and the dissolved yeast. Mix well, then add additional flour; knead. Let rise until more than doubled in bulk.

Form the dough into balls of 2 sizes—1 the size of a walnut, the other slightly larger. Place the larger on the pan and the smaller one on top of it. Let rise. Bake at 410 degrees 20 to 25 minutes.

Chili Rice Hot Dish

Cook 1 cup rice in salted water until partially done. Fry gently 1½ pounds hamburger, season with salt, pepper, Loery's seasoning, and dash of chili powder.

Add 2 medium-sized onions, chopped. When onions are cooked through, add 1 can of kidney beans (drained) and 1 cup of chopped celery.

Grease a fair-sized casserole and alternate the meat mixture with the drained cooked rice. Over it all pour 1 quart of tomato juice or V8 juice. Bake at 350 degrees for 1 hour or more.

Frozen Berry Dessert

1½ cups vanilla wafers, crushed
½ cup butter
1½ cups powdered sugar
1 teaspoon vanilla
2 eggs
1 cup whipping cream, whipped
1 package frozen raspberries (or
   2 cups fresh berries)
½ cup chopped nuts, if desired

Put 1 cup of crumbs into bottom of 9" x 13" pan. Cream butter and powdered sugar. Add vanilla and eggs, one at a time. Beat well. Place over crumbs in pan.

Whip the cream until it holds peaks and add partially thawed berries. Pour this over mixture in the pan and sprinkle rest of the wafer mixture and nuts on top. Place in refrigerator overnight. (Crisp leftover cookies may be crushed and used instead of vanilla wafers.)

Fruit Soup (German)

½ cup sago
1 cup prunes
½ cup raisins
½ orange
½ lemon
½ gallon boiling water
1 cup diced apple
1 cup grape juice

Sweeten to taste and cook 45 minutes, stirring occasionally.

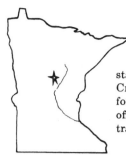

CROW WING COUNTY a resort leader, got an early start in the business. When Allan Morrison settled at Crow Wing in 1843, he made his house a "stopping place" for travelers. A decade later a few enterprising settlers offered to sell or rent camp outfits and provide guides so travelers could see "the wilds of America."

Rabbit à la Mode

1 rabbit
Water, vinegar
1 onion
½ teaspoon salt
6 peppercorns
1 bay leaf
Salt, pepper, flour
3 tablespoons fat
Sweet or sour cream

Clean rabbit and cut into small pieces. Place in crock or jar. Cover with vinegar and water in equal parts. Add onion, salt, peppercorns, and bay leaf. Soak rabbit for 2 days, then remove meat, keeping the liquid.

Sprinkle with salt and pepper and roll in flour. Brown in fat, pour in vinegar water to the depth of ¼". Cover tightly and simmer until done. Do not boil at any time.

Remove rabbit from pot, thicken drippings and add sweet or sour cream to gravy.

Lemon Sticks

½ cup butter
½ cup powdered sugar
2 egg yolks
1 cup flour
2 teaspoons lemon rind, grated

Cream butter and powdered sugar; add yolks, beat until light. Stir in flour and lemon rind. Mix until smooth and spread in 13" x 9" pan, ungreased. Bake 10 minutes at 350 degrees.

Spread meringue over mixture and bake 25 minutes more. Cool and cut.

Meringue

2 egg whites, beaten stiff
½ cup sugar
1 tablespoon lemon juice
½ cup nuts, chopped

Potica

Dough

**2 cakes compressed yeast or
2 packages active dry yeast**
¼ cup lukewarm water
2 cups milk, scalded
2 teaspoons salt
¼ cup sugar
¼ cup butter
2 eggs, well beaten
8 cups sifted enriched flour

Soften yeast in water. In the meantime scald the milk. Combine hot milk, salt, sugar, and butter. Blend thoroughly. Cool to lukewarm. Add eggs and softened yeast. Blend thoroughly. Sift 6 cups of the flour into a large bowl. Gradually add milk mixture, beating vigorously. This makes a sticky dough. Gradually add remaining 2 cups of flour or enough of it to make a medium soft dough. Place in a large greased bowl. Cover with a damp cloth. Let rise in a warm place until double in bulk, about 2 hours.

Walnut Filling

1 cup milk
1 pound ground walnuts
3 eggs, unbeaten
1 cup honey
½ cup sugar

Scald milk over low heat in heavy skillet. (Be sure it is heavy, as filling burns easily.) Add nuts. Let mixture come to a boil, stirring constantly. Add eggs one at a time, beating constantly. Combine honey and sugar. Blend thoroughly. Gradually add to milk mixture, stirring constantly. Cook over low heat 5 minutes. Remove from heat. Cool. Cover a 38″ x 60″ table with a white cloth (a sheet will do), being sure that the cloth is larger than the table. Lightly flour the cloth. Place raised dough on center of cloth.

Pull dough gently until it more than covers the table, at least by 1 ″. The dough should be paper-thin. If it tears, pull it together and patch it. Cut off all dough that is hanging over the table so that you will have a perfect oblong with ends and sides trimmed as evenly as possible. Spread the filling evenly but thinly on the dough, covering every inch. Form dough in a roll by lifting the end of the cloth and rolling the dough evenly over and over and over. Do not work too rapidly.

Put roll into a greased 10″ x 13″ pan, forming it in an S. Be sure that the parts of the S are pushed closely together. Cover with a large piece of waxed paper. Cover waxed paper with a cloth. Let dough rise in a warm place until double in bulk, about 2 hours. Prick dough in 10 to 12 places on top and sides. Bake in hot oven (400 degrees) for 1 hour.

DAKOTA COUNTY snug between the Minnesota and Mississippi rivers, thrived early. LeSueur built an island fort there before 1700. Mendota was a busy capital of a vast fur empire before Minnesota was a territory. Henry Sibley, later governor, arrived in 1834 and within a year shipped out more than 400,000 pelts.

Aunt Mary's Rham Kuchen

1 package rolled Holland rusk
½ cup sugar
¼ cup butter
½ teaspoon cinnamon
2 pounds cottage cheese (dry)
1 cup sugar
4 eggs, beat yolks and whites separately
   Salt to taste
2 tablespoons flour
½ pint whipping cream, whipped
   Juice and grated rind of one lemon

Melt butter and mix with rusk, sugar, and cinnamon. Pat into spring-form pan, pushing a bit up the sides. Reserve ½ cup crumb mixture for top.

Mix remaining ingredients in order named, and lastly fold in egg whites and whipped cream gently but thoroughly. Bake 1 hour at 350 degrees. Turn off oven and let torte remain in oven another 15 to 30 minutes.

Soft Molasses Cookies

5 cups flour
2 teaspoons soda
3 teaspoons ginger
1 teaspoon cinnamon
¼ teaspoon cloves
   Dash of salt
2 cups molasses
1 cup shortening
½ cup sugar, white or brown
2 eggs, beaten

Sift flour, measure and sift again with spices. Add molasses, shortening, sugar, and eggs. Then add 1 cup hot water with 1 more teaspoon soda. Mix well and chill. When ready to roll and cut out, add just enough extra flour to be able to handle. Bake in 375 degree oven 10 to 12 minutes. Bake just until set but not hard.

Auntie's Oatmeal Bread

This recipe dates back to World War I when we were first rationed in sugar and when, for every 10 pounds of wheat flour, we also had to buy some other cereal grain and we were asked to make breads, muffins, etc., with a mixture of flours. We thought this recipe was delicious then, and it is still a favorite now three generations hence. Agnes Karpen, Hastings.

2 cups oatmeal
1 quart water, boiling
1 cake compressed yeast
¼ cup lukewarm water
3½ cups sifted flour
½ cup shortening
½ cup sugar
½ cup syrup
5 cups flour, approximate
1 cup chopped walnuts

Scald oatmeal in boiling water and cool to lukewarm. Soak yeast in lukewarm water and add to oatmeal mixture together with flour. Set in warm place until sponge is doubled in bulk.

Melt shortening, add sugar and syrup. When cool, add to sponge and add enough sifted flour in order to be able to knead dough. Add chopped nuts and knead until it no longer sticks to hands. Let rise twice and then place in bread tins. Makes 3 loaves. Bake 1 hour at 350 degrees.

Hot Potato Salad (German)

1 pound (3 medium) potatoes
3 slices bacon, diced
1 medium-sized onion, diced
¼ to ½ cup vinegar
1 cup water
2 tablespoons flour
1 teaspoon sugar
Salt and pepper to taste

Scrub potatoes, rinse, boil in jackets. Let cool. Cook bacon in frying pan until crisp. Remove the bacon cubes to a dish. Add flour to bacon grease and blend well. Stir in vinegar and water and cook until thickened. Stir constantly.

Peel and slice potatoes, add onion. Gently mix them into the thickened gravy, permitting the potatoes to heat thoroughly on low heat. Season to taste, add the cubed bacon pieces. Serve with garnish of hard-boiled eggs.

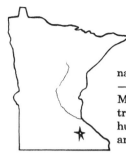

DODGE COUNTY was hungry after a cruel trick of nature in the year Minnesota became a state. Hailstones —some measuring 15 inches around—rained down near Mantorville on July 30, killing hogs and chickens and destroying crops. So severe was the damage that several hundred dollars was borrowed in New York to buy food and supplies.

Lemon Sponge (Amish)

2½ cups sifted cake flour
1 teaspoon salt
⅔ cup shortening
⅓ cup cold water, approximately

Measure sifted flour, add salt and sift again. Cut in shortening with pastry blender. Sprinkle with water and mix lightly with fork. Press into ball and roll out on lightly floured board ⅛" thick; makes enough for two 9" shells.

Filling for one 9" unbaked shell

2 tablespoons butter
1 cup sugar
3 eggs, separated
3 tablespoons flour
½ teaspoon salt
Juice and grated rind of one lemon
1½ cups hot milk

Cream butter, add sugar, and egg yolks. Beat until light and fluffy. Stir in flour, salt, lemon juice, and rind. Add hot milk, fold in stiffly-beaten egg whites.

Bake in hot oven (400 degrees) about 40 minutes.

Strawberry Party Cookies

1 pound coconut, ground fine
¼ pound blanched almonds, ground fine
2 tablespoons white sugar
2 boxes strawberry Jello (reserve ½ box)
½ teaspoon almond extract
1 cup evaporated milk

Mix above ingredients well. Shape a small amount into a strawberry and roll in the ½ box of strawberry Jello which has been mixed with 4 tablespoons of sugar and a little red coloring. Make colored leaves of powdered sugar. Don't bake.

Cherry Crunch

40 graham crackers, rolled fine
¾ cup sugar
1 teaspoon cinnamon
1¼ cups butter
1 quart cherries
1¼ cups sugar
5 tablespoons cornstarch
5 egg whites, stiffly beaten
¾ cup sugar

Melt butter, mix cracker crumbs, sugar, and cinnamon. Pat ¾ mixture in bottom and sides of large buttered pan. Mix cornstarch and 1¼ cups sugar, add to cherries. Cook until thickened and clear, stirring constantly. Pour over crumb mixture in pan. Beat egg whites until stiff, add ¾ cup sugar. Spread this mixture over cherries. Cover with remaining crumb mixture and bake 35 minutes at 275 degrees. Cut in large squares. Serve with plain or whipped cream or ice cream. This can be made the day before.

Dixie Crumb Cake

½ cup shortening
1 cup sugar
2 cups flour
1 teaspoon nutmeg
1 teaspoon cloves
1 teaspoon cinnamon
1 tablespoon molasses
1 cup sour milk
1 teaspoon soda

Mix shortening, sugar, flour, nutmeg, cloves, and cinnamon into crumbly mixture similar to pie crust. Save out 1 cup of this mixture. To the rest add the molasses, sour milk, and soda. Mix well and pour into well-greased large cake pan. Sprinkle the cup of crumbs over the top. Bake 30 minutes at 375 degrees.

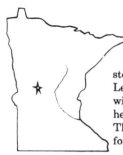

DOUGLAS COUNTY home of the Kensington rune stone, once was fought over by Sioux and Chippewa. Legend tells of Neewana, a Sioux maiden, who fell in love with a Chippewa but was pledged to marry a Sioux. When her lover was killed, she threw herself into Lake Geneva. The story says each year a lovely blue flower blooms there for just one day.

Avocado Salad

1 cup water
1 teaspoon onion juice
1 teaspoon lemon juice
1 package lime Jello
2 tablespoons green pepper, chopped fine
½ cup celery, chopped fine
1 avocado, diced
½ cup mayonnaise
½ cup cream, whipped

Boil water, onion juice, and lemon juice. Pour over Jello. When congealed, add remaining ingredients. Mold in ring. Fill center with sections of oranges, grapefruit, and avocado, which have been marinated in French dressing.

Crabs in Coquilles

4 tablespoons butter
1 green pepper, chopped
1 tablespoon minced onion
4 tablespoons flour
1 cup stock or chicken soup
1 cup cream
1 large can crab meat or 2 small ones
½ pound mushrooms, or 1 large can
1 tablespoon lemon juice
4 hard-cooked eggs, chopped
1 small can pimiento
1 or 2 tablespoons sherry

Fry the onion, mushrooms, and green pepper in the butter; add the flour, cream, and stock to make a thick sauce. Pour the lemon juice over crab meat; let stand while preparing the sauce. Add all remaining ingredients to the sauce. Season well. Let cool before putting in greased shells. Cover with buttered crumbs and bake about 20 minutes or until crumbs are brown. For variation, add grated American or Parmesan cheese to the crumbs.

Tuna Cashew Casserole

1 No. 2½ can chow mein noodles
1 can condensed mushroom soup
½ cup hot water
1 can chunk style tuna
¼ pound cashew nuts
1 cup finely-chopped celery
¼ cup minced onion
Pepper and salt to taste

Save ½ cup noodles for top. Mix all ingredients and place in casserole. Sprinkle extra noodles over top. Bake 40 minutes in 325 degree oven.

Knute Nelson Bean Soup

This well-known soup is now featured in the Senate Restaurant in Washington, D.C.

Take 3 pounds small navy pea beans, wash and rinse in hot water until beans are white. Add 4 quarts hot water, then add 1½ pounds smoked ham hocks; boil for 2½ hours. Braise chopped onion in butter until light brown; add to soup, season with salt and pepper. Do not salt until ready to serve. This makes 8 servings.

Red Devil Franks

1 pound frankfurters or wieners (8 to 10)
4 tablespoons butter, or salad oil
1 cup finely-chopped onions
2 cloves garlic, minced
½ teaspoon salt
⅛ teaspoon pepper
1½ tablespoons Worcestershire sauce
1½ tablespoons prepared mustard
1½ teaspoons sugar
½ cup chili sauce

Cook onion and garlic in fat over low heat until onion is tender (10 minutes). Add all other ingredients. Continue heating until flavors are well blended (about 5 minutes). Split wieners lengthwise, arrange in shallow pan; spoon sauce over them and heat under broiler.

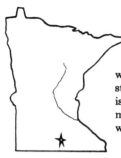

FARIBAULT COUNTY'S name is that of a fur trader who was, perhaps, the first permanent white settler in the state. Jean Baptisté Faribault set up housekeeping on an island in what is now Dakota county. Twice forced to move by high waters, he finally built a house in 1826 where Mendota now is. History records no earlier settler.

Sweet and Sour Pork

This is my favorite Oriental dish; it was a gift from a group of Okinawan women with whom we American servicemen's wives exchanged recipes. Mrs. William Stokman, Minnesota Lake.

> 10 ounces boneless pork loin, cubed
> 1 beaten egg
> ½ teaspoon salt
> Dash of pepper
> Few drops sesame oil
> 4 tablespoons cornstarch
> 4 tablespoons vinegar
> 4 tablespoons water
> 1 tablespoon catsup
> 2 tablespoons soy sauce
> Few drops of sesame oil
> Dash of pepper
> 4 tablespoons sugar
> 1 good-sized tomato, cubed
> ½ small green pepper, cut up
> ½ onion
> Scallions
> Pineapple chunks, ⅓ can
> 1 medium cucumber

Fry the pork until well cooked in deep fat fryer at 400 degrees. Remove and add egg, salt, pepper, sesame oil, and cornstarch. In a sauce pan mix the vinegar, water, catsup, soy sauce, sesame oil, pepper, and sugar. Add the vegetables and fruit to this sauce and cook slowly until tomatoes are soft (not mushy). Add meat mixture and serve at once on toast.

Crank Freezer Ice Cream

5 cups milk
5 cups cream
5 eggs
3 cups sugar
1½ tablespoons flour
2 teaspoons vanilla

Heat 4 cups of the milk to almost boiling. Add sugar and flour mixed together. Cook until boiling. Add lightly-beaten egg yolks; strain. Cool this mixture very thoroughly. Add 1 more cup milk and the cream. Add the vanilla and beaten egg whites. Freeze as follows.

Place can in freezer tub. Put dasher in place. Fill can ⅔ full. Cover, adjust crank. Fill freezer tub ⅓ full of crushed ice. Add remaining crushed ice alternately with layers of coarse salt. Let mixture stand in ice-packed freezer about 5 minutes before turning crank. Turn slowly at first (5 to 10 minutes), to insure smooth, fine-grained ice cream. Then turn rapidly until crank turns with difficulty. Draw off water. Wipe off and remove lid. Take out dasher. Plug opening in lid. Pack mixture down. Repack in ice and salt. Cover with heavy cloth. Let ripen several hours. Makes 1 gallon.

Whole Wheat Bread

3 cups liquid
2 tablespoons salt
3 tablespoons sugar
3 tablespoons fat
2 cakes yeast
3 quarts whole wheat flour

The liquid used may be milk, milk and water, or potato water. A good combination is ⅓ cup milk and ⅔ cup water. Scald milk, add water and let cool to lukewarm. Break up yeast and soften in ½ cup of liquid. Add remaining liquid, salt, sugar, and fat. Add flour, mixing thoroughly, until dough is soft enough to be conveniently handled, but not sticky. A little more or less flour may be needed, according to the kind of flour or liquid used. Knead dough thoroughly, until smooth and elastic; form into ball and put in bowl to rise. Cover with a piece of moist cheese cloth to prevent cracking.

When dough has risen to double its bulk, in about 1½ hours, knead again and let rise as before. Divide dough, mold into loaves, and place in oiled pans for last rising. Brush top of each loaf with a little melted fat. When loaves have risen to twice their original size, put in hot oven (400 degrees). After the first 10 to 15 minutes, turn loaves around to even the baking, reduce heat to moderate 350 degrees and continue baking until done, 45 to 60 minutes in all.

FILLMORE COUNTY had a puzzle some 30 years ago. One of its farmers kept losing his pigs. There were no clues until, walking through an open field, he heard faint grunts and squeals. Following the sound, he came to an opening in the ground and found his pigs in a cavern that now, as Niagara cave, is a tourist attraction.

Tuna Rice Casserole

¾ cup rice (soak overnight and drain in morning)
1 can cream of mushroom soup
1 can water
1 can cream of chicken soup
1 can water
1 can mushrooms, diced
1 can tuna
1 onion, minced
1 can pimiento, diced
⅓ bunch celery, chopped
¼ pound almonds, blanched and chopped

Mix in large casserole. Bake 1½ to 2 hours at 350 degrees. Stir occasionally.

Filled Oatmeal Cookies

1 cup sugar
1 cup butter, part lard
2 cups oatmeal, ground until flour-like
½ cup sour milk
1 teaspoon soda
Flour, about 3 to 4 cups

Mix the ingredients together and use enough of the flour so the cookies can be rolled out very thin. Bake in moderate oven (350 degrees). Remove from pans and when cool spread the date filling and top with another cookie. These make very delicious sandwich cookies.

Filling

1 package dates, ground
1 cup sugar
1 cup water

Cook the ground dates, sugar, and water until thick. When cool, spread on cookies.

Chocolate Chip Cake

1 cup dates, finely cut
1 cup hot water
1 teaspoon soda
1 cup white sugar
1 cup shortening
2 eggs
2 cups flour, sifted
1 tablespoon cocoa
¼ teaspoon salt
1 tablespoon vanilla
1 small bag chocolate chips
1 cup finely cut nuts

Combine hot water, dates, and soda. Let stand ½ hour.

Mix sugar, shortening, eggs, and vanilla and add to above ingredients.

Sift flour, cocoa, salt, and add to above. Add ¼ cup of the chocolate chips and ⅓ cup nuts. Pour into large greased loaf pan.

Sprinkle rest of bag of chocolate chips and ⅔ cup nuts on top and bake about 40 minutes in 350 degree oven.

Chicken Tetrazzini

2 cups cooked, boned chicken
1 8-ounce package spaghetti
2 chicken bouillon cubes
¼ teaspoon pepper
¼ teaspoon rosemary
3 tablespoons salad oil
2 tablespoons flour
1 4-ounce can mushrooms
½ cup blanched almonds
1 cup milk or cream
2 tablespoons sherry
Parmesan cheese, grated

Cut chicken into bite-sized chunks. Cook spaghetti until tender in 2 quarts boiling water with 1 tablespoon salt. Drain. Dissolve bouillon cubes in 2 cups water, add pepper and rosemary. Heat oil, blend in flour. Gradually add bouillon, cook and stir until thickened. Remove from heat, add chicken, spaghetti, mushrooms, almonds, milk or cream, and sherry. Add salt to taste. Put in greased casserole, sprinkle with cheese. Bake in a moderate oven (350 degrees) 20 minutes or until brown. Serves 8.

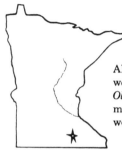

FREEBORN COUNTY wrangled over the county seat, at Albert Lea. Nearby Itasca set up a horse race between well-bred *Itasca Fly* and the sheriff's homely *Old Tom*. *Old Tom's* rooters "borrowed" *Itasca Fly* one night for a moonlit trial heat. Next day, with heavy bets, *Old Tom* won. Itasca people, flat broke, then supported Albert Lea.

Olie Bolen (Dutch doughnut)

3 eggs, beaten
1 cup sugar   .
1 teaspoon soda
1 pound currants
2 cups buttermilk
½ teaspoon vanilla
2½ cups flour (scant)

Prepare hot fat as for doughnuts. Mix ingredients in order listed. The dough should be a little thicker than for a white cake. Drop mixture by spoonfuls into hot fat, fry until golden brown.

Pumpkin or Squash Rolls

1 cup baked pumpkin or squash puree
½ cup white sugar
1½ teaspoons salt
1 cup scalded milk
1 cake yeast
¼ cup lukewarm water
½ cup melted shortening
2 teaspoons lemon rind, grated
5 cups flour

Combine pumpkin or squash pulp, sugar, salt, and hot milk. Beat until smooth and lukewarm. Mix yeast with lukewarm water; add to pulp mixture. Add melted shortening and lemon rind. Blend well. Add about ½ the sifted flour. Beat into smooth batter. Add remaining flour to make a soft dough. Mix well. Cover and let rise in a warm place until double in bulk. Cover dough with waxed paper and towel.

Chill overnight in refrigerator. When ready to use, shape into small balls, place in greased muffin tins. Grease rolls and cut with clover leaf press. Let rise in warm place until double in bulk.

Bake at 375 degrees for 25 or 30 minutes. Brush tops of rolls with melted fat immediately after baking. When cool, frost.

Grandmother's Cream of Chicken Soup

A really good soup is a lost art that belonged to grandmother's day. This is one to be remembered. Mrs. Harold Mueller, Albert Lea.

1 4-pound chicken
1 veal knuckle
2 tablespoons chicken fat
1 onion, sliced
2 large carrots, quartered
2½ quarts cold water
4 sprigs parsley
2 stalks celery
1 teaspoon salt
4 peppercorns
1 cup cream
2 tablespoons flour
2 egg yolks
Salt to taste

Cut up chicken as for frying; cut up veal into small pieces. Heat the fat in a heavy soup pot and very slightly brown the pieces of chicken, the knuckle, onion, and carrots. Add water and bring slowly to a boil. Skim off the top and add remaining vegetables plus 1 teaspoon of salt and peppercorns. Simmer for 2 hours.

Remove the pieces of breast and cover them with a little of the broth. Continue cooking the soup for another 3 hours.

Strain, cool, and skim off every particle of grease. Reheat soup and return the breast meat, chopped.

Mix cream and flour together until smooth, add egg yolks and heat thoroughly. Strain the mixture into the simmering soup and let thicken for 3 minutes, stirring constantly. Serves 8.

Mexican Luncheon

1 pound bulk pork sausage
1 cup onion, diced
1 cup green pepper, diced
2 cups tomatoes
2 cups sour cream
2 cups uncooked macaroni
2 tablespoons sugar
1 tablespoon chili powder (scant)
1 teaspoon salt

Brown sausage, onions, and green pepper. Add tomatoes, sour cream, macaroni, and seasonings. Cover. Simmer 20 minutes. Makes 8 servings.

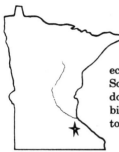

GOODHUE COUNTY borders the Mississippi, with its echoes of French explorers and, later, brawny lumberjacks. South of Red Wing, named for the Sioux chief Whoo-pa-doo-to (Wing of Scarlet), the river now draws scores of bird watchers. It's one of the best spots on the continent to study bird migrations.

Walnut Cookies

1 cup shortening (half butter)
½ cup granulated sugar
½ cup brown sugar, packed
1 egg
1 teaspoon vanilla
2 cups flour
½ teaspoon soda
½ teaspoon salt
½ cup walnuts, chopped

Cream shortening and sugars. Add egg, vanilla, dry ingredients, and walnuts. Roll into balls size of walnut; dip balls into granulated sugar. Flatten with glass. Place on greased cookie sheet. Bake about 10 minutes or until delicate brown at 375 degrees.

Toll House Cookies with Oatmeal

1 cup shortening
¾ cup white sugar
¾ cup brown sugar
2 eggs
1½ cups flour
1 teaspoon soda
1 teaspoon salt
2 cups oatmeal
1 teaspoon vanilla
½ cup nut meats

Cream shortening, sugars, and eggs. Sift flour, soda, and salt together and add to creamed mixture. Add remaining ingredients, drop by teaspoon on greased cookie sheet. Bake at 375 degrees for about 8 minutes.

Mock Chow Mein

1 pound hamburger
1 small onion, chopped
1 cup celery, chopped
2 tablespoons soy sauce
½ cup rice
1 can cream of mushroom soup
1 can water (soup can)
1 4-ounce can mushrooms

Brown hamburger in small amount of fat in skillet. Put remaining ingredients into casserole, using soy sauce instead of salt for seasoning. Add hamburger. Bake at least 1 hour at 350 degrees. Serves 4 to 6.

Julekage (Swedish Christmas bread)

2 cakes compressed yeast
½ cup lukewarm water
2 teaspoons sugar
1½ cups scalded milk
½ cup butter
½ cup sugar
2 teaspoons salt
2 eggs, beaten
½ teaspoon cardamom seed, crushed
7 cups flour
½ cup citron, chopped
½ cup raisins
½ cup chopped candied cherries or one
    package of mixed candied fruits

Dissolve yeast in water with 2 teaspoons of sugar. Scald milk and pour over the butter, sugar, and salt. When cooled, add the yeast, eggs, cardamom, and 3 cups of the flour. Beat well. Gradually mix in the rest of the flour by kneading on floured board when dough is too stiff to handle with spoon. This dough should be firm enough to mold into loaves but not as heavy as regular bread dough.

Let rise until double in bulk. Knead in the fruits and let rise again. Mold into loaves. Let rise and bake 40 to 45 minutes at 350 degrees.

This bread burns easily so heat may have to be reduced. After removing from oven, spread with thin powdered sugar icing. Yield: 3 medium loaves.

GRANT COUNTY was named for the Civil War general who was president when the county was organized, in 1871. The county seat was set up in Elbow Lake, near old Fort Pomme De Terre. These days, the county seat is still Elbow Lake, despite a long-ago, dark-of-night raid when residents of nearby Herman carried off the records.

Prune Dessert

1¼ cups sugar
½ cup butter
2 eggs, beaten
¾ cup cooked prunes, cut up
¼ cup prune juice
½ cup sour cream
1 teaspoon soda (in cream)
½ teaspoon salt
1 teaspoon cinnamon
1 teaspoon vanilla
2 cups flour

Cream sugar and butter, add well-beaten eggs, prunes cut up, prune juice, and sour cream with soda and vanilla. Mix well. Add dry ingredients which have been sifted together. Bake in a 14"x10" pan in 350 degree oven until cake breaks away from pan. Top with dressing.

Dressing
1 cup sugar
3 tablespoons flour
¾ cup sour cream
1 tablespoon butter
1 egg
½ cup cooked prunes
1½ teaspoons vanilla
½ cup dates, cut up
½ cup nut meats

Mix ingredients and cook in double boiler, stirring constantly until thickened. Cool and spread over cooled cake. Cut cake in squares and serve with whipped cream on top. Serves 15 to 18 people.

Braised Venison Sour Cream

2 pounds solid venison
¼ cup bacon fat
1 clove garlic, peeled
1 cup celery, diced
1 cup carrots, diced
½ cup onion, minced
2 cups water
1 cup grapefruit juice
1 bay leaf
8 peppercorns
1 teaspoon salt
4 tablespoons butter
4 tablespoons flour
1 cup sour cream

Cut venison in 2" pieces. Melt bacon fat in heavy skillet, add meat, and garlic, and saute until brown on all sides. Arrange meat in 2-quart casserole. Put vegetables in skillet and cook 2 minutes in remaining bacon fat. Add water, juice, bay leaf, peppercorns, and salt. Pour this mixture over venison, cover and bake in slow oven (325 degrees) 30 to 60 minutes, until meat is tender.

Melt butter in frying pan, stir in flour. When well blended, add the liquid in which meat has been cooked, stirring constantly until mixture thickens and boils. Add sour cream and more salt, if needed. Pour over venison and vegetables in casserole. Serve immediately with buttered noodles and tart cranberries or jelly.

Eggs Heidelberg

Place small slices of lettuce, fresh tomato, boiled ham in a pile, one on top of the other on the plate. Secure a hard-boiled egg on the top with a toothpick. Cover with Thousand Island Dressing. This is a good main dish for a luncheon. Use 2 or 3 slices of each.

Thousand Island Dressing

3 egg yolks
2 cups cooking oil
Salt
Cayenne pepper
Drop Tabasco sauce
Malt vinegar as needed after the
    mixture is well started

Make a mayonnaise of the above. Then add:

1 cup chili sauce (not home made)
3 hard-boiled eggs, chopped fine
2 pimientos, chopped (canned)

HENNEPIN COUNTY is named for the Belgian friar, Father Louis Hennepin, who found and named the Falls of St. Anthony in 1680. Another early explorer described the sound of the giant falls as "that of thunder rolling in the air." The falls determined the location of the state's biggest city, now Minneapolis, which grew up around the mills powered by the falls.

Pennsylvania Dutch Salad Dressing

    ½ **pound bacon**
    2 **eggs**
    1 **tablespoon salt**
    5 **tablespoons sugar**
    ½ **cup vinegar**
    ½ **cup water**
    ½ **cup cream**

Cut bacon in tiny pieces and fry out in saucepan. Set aside half the fried bacon. Beat the eggs, add the salt, sugar, vinegar, and water. Beat well and add to the bacon and the bacon fat in the saucepan. Heat slowly, beating constantly until the mixture thickens. Remove from the fire and add the cream.

Pour this over head lettuce, garden lettuce or field salad. Garnish with the additional bacon and some hard-cooked egg.

Lothrop Family Apple Pie

This recipe was passed on to me from my husband's family and came originally from his great-grandmother. The Lothrops homesteaded near Zumbrota about 1850. This has been a family favorite for many generations and still is a favorite with my children. Mrs. Orville L. Freeman, Minneapolis.

Butter a pie tin. Fill it with sliced, red Minnesota apples. Sprinkle ½ cup white sugar over the apples and top with following mixture. Bake at 350 degrees until apples are done.

    Topping
    ½ **cup butter**
    ¾ **cup brown sugar**
    1 **cup flour**

Mix together into crumbs and spread over apples.

Kolaches

2 cakes yeast
2 cups scalded milk
   (cool to lukewarm)
2 eggs, well beaten
½ cup sugar
¼ teaspoon mace
¾ cup shortening (use half butter)
7 cups flour
1½ teaspoons salt

Dissolve yeast in ¼ cup lukewarm water. Combine with cooled milk, eggs, sugar, mace, shortening, and salt. Add flour. Beat dough until light. Put in greased bowl. Let rise to twice its size in a warm place. Punch down, turn over in the bowl. Let rise again until almost double in bulk. Punch down. Place on lightly-floured board or canvas. Allow to rest 10 minutes. Roll dough from ⅛″ to ¼″ thick. Cut into 3″ squares or cut pieces and pull into 3″ squares. Place spoonful of filling on each. Fold opposite corners to center and pinch together. Place in greased pans 2″ apart. Let rise until light, not quite double, though, 30 to 40 minutes. Bake at 375 degrees for 20 to 25 minutes or until golden brown.

Prune or Apricot Filling

1½ cups chopped cooked prunes or apricots
¼ cup fruit juice
½ cup sugar
1 tablespoon lemon juice
½ teaspoon cinnamon
¼ teaspoon cloves (optional)

Cinnamon Apple Filling

4 small apples, peeled and chopped
3 tablespoons cinnamon candies or
   1 teaspoon cinnamon
⅓ cup water
Sugar to taste (about ¼ cup)

Cook together until soft; drain and press pulp through sieve.

Poppy Seed Filling

½ cup poppy seed, crushed or ground
⅓ cup cream
1 tablespoon butter
1 tablespoon honey
2 tablespoons sugar
1 tablespoon cornstarch
2 tablespoons red jelly

Boil together 1 minute, then cool. Makes 1½ cups filling.

HOUSTON COUNTY blames Jacob Webster, who came to Caledonia in 1854, for the abundance of dandelions in the state. Webster, hungering for greens, sent to New England for dandelion seed, which grew all too willingly in the fertile Minnesota soil. Beneath the dandelions are many caves, once Indian tombs and now important historic sites and a tourist attraction.

Pineapple Crisscross Coffee Cake

2 packages yeast, compressed or dry
¼ cup lukewarm water
1 cup milk
½ cup sugar
2 teaspoons salt
¼ cup shortening
5 cups sifted flour (about)
2 eggs
1 teaspoon grated lemon rind
Melted butter
Pineapple Coconut Filling
1 egg white, slightly beaten
½ cup slivered, blanched almonds

Soften yeast in water. Scald milk. Add sugar, salt, and shortening. Cool to lukewarm. Add about 2 cups flour to make thick batter. Mix well. Add softened yeast, eggs, and lemon rind. Beat well. Add enough more flour to make soft dough.

Turn out on lightly floured board or pastry cloth and knead until smooth and satiny. Place in greased bowl, cover and let rise until doubled. When light, punch down.

Let rest 10 minutes. Divide into three portions. Roll each portion to rectangle about 8" x 12". Place on greased baking sheet. Brush dough with butter.

Spread Pineapple Coconut Filling lengthwise on center third of each dough. With scissors or sharp knife, make cuts 2" in from side at 1" intervals on unspread portions of dough.

Alternately fold strips over filling. Let rise until doubled. Brush top with egg white and sprinkle with almonds. Bake in moderate oven (350 degrees) 25 to 30 minutes. Makes three coffee cakes.

Pineapple Coconut Filling

2¼ cups crushed pineapple
(1 lb. 4 oz. can)
1 cup toasted flaked coconut
¼ teaspoon cinnamon

Combine ingredients and mix well. Spread down center of dough.

Fowl Dressing

10 cups bread crumbs (dry or
slightly toasted)

6 medium-sized apples (Northwestern
Greenings are favorites)

1½ cups raisins

¼ cup sugar (scant)

Seasonings of salt, cinnamon,
cloves, and poultry seasoning

Giblets

Cook giblets and any part of the neck that is to be cut off before roasting in about 2 cups water and a little salt. Cook until tender. Cool. Cut meat into small pieces. Peel the apples, quarter, core, and slice thin. Combine the bread crumbs, apples, raisins (well plumped), sugar, and seasonings, with the cooked meat cubes. If the bird is not very fat, add a generous tablespoon of butter to the meat stock. Combine with the first mixture, adding only enough of the liquid so it is thoroughly moistened. Fill the cavities of the bird in the usual way. This dressing is for about a 10-pound bird.

Salmon Puff

6 slices bread

1 tall can salmon

2 cups milk

3 eggs

Salt to taste

Cut bread into triangles. Cover bottom of square baking pan with half of bread. Flake salmon and put over layer of bread. Cover with remaining bread. Beat eggs with the milk and salt. Pour over salmon mixture. Let stand ½ hour. Bake in moderate oven 45 minutes. Serve with canned, thickened peas as a sauce.

Lickin' Good Hot Dish

Slice thinly about 8 medium-sized potatoes in baking dish. Season each layer with salt and pepper to taste. Cover with layer of thinly-sliced onion. Season. Add 1 No. 2 can cream style corn. Form 1 pound seasoned pork sausage in balls the size of walnuts and put on top of corn. Pour over 1 can tomato soup. Bake in moderate oven (350 degrees) 1 hour covered and ½ hour uncovered, to brown.

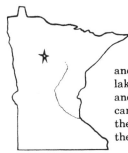

HUBBARD COUNTY'S 365 lakes have 18 varieties of fish and some of the best names in the state. There's Ham lake and Potato lake. Spider and Skunk. Little Mantrap and Bad Axe. A civil engineer named Thomas B. Walker came to the pine forests on a land survey. He mapped the timber areas in his spare time and made a fortune in the lumbering business.

Venison Chasseur

1 4- to 6-pound venison roast
1 cup claret wine
1 cup water
1½ teaspoons salt
1 bay leaf
10 whole cloves and allspice
6 peppercorns or 2 chilis
1 medium-sized onion, sliced

Mix together wine, water, salt, bay leaf, cloves, allspice, peppercorns or chilis, and onion. Pour sauce over venison roast and marinate for two days. Remove meat from sauce, dry well and brown on all sides in 2 tablespoons fat. Add ¼ cup of chopped onion, ½ cup wine, cover and simmer for two to three hours. Add water to roast as needed. Strain remaining sauce used for marinating and add to roast during last 15 minutes of cooking. Remove roast, thicken gravy with flour and water paste. Serve gravy over thick slices of venison roast.

Apple Bread (Dutch)

This bread freezes well. Is delicious sliced thin and spread with butter and favorite jam or cheese.

½ cup shortening (not butter)
1 cup sugar
1½ tablespoons sour milk
2 eggs, beaten
1 teaspoon vanilla
2 cups sifted flour
1 teaspoon soda
1 teaspoon orange extract
¼ teaspoon salt
1 cup coarsely-chopped apple, peeled

Mix, divide into two 4" x 8" pans, top with 2 teaspoons sugar and 1 teaspoon cinnamon and bake 1 hour in moderate oven (350 degrees).

Baked Northern Pike

1 4-pound Northern pike
1 medium-sized onion, chopped
4 tablespoons butter
2 cups thick sour cream
1 cup tomato soup
Salt and pepper

Place well-seasoned cleaned fish (skin left on) in roaster. Brown onion in butter and put into fish cavity. Mix cream and soup in pan in which onion was browned, heat and pour over fish. Bake 45 minutes in very hot oven (425 degrees), basting frequently. Serve with the sauce poured over it.

Old-fashioned Buckwheat Pancakes

3½ cups old-fashioned buckwheat flour
1 cup white flour
1 package yeast
4 cups lukewarm water
1 teaspoon sugar
1 teaspoon salt

Mix and let stand overnight at room temperature, in a large bowl to allow room for rising. In the morning add:

2 teaspoons brown sugar
⅔ teaspoon soda
1 tablespoon melted fat

Remaining batter may be kept in refrigerator and brought out the night before wanted, the amount increased by adding 1 cup of lukewarm water for each cup buckwheat flour, and salt in proportion to above.

Egg Foam Dumplings

2 egg yolks, well beaten
3 tablespoons flour
2 egg whites, stiffly beaten

Combine beaten yolks and flour and beat until smooth. Fold into stiffly-beaten whites and drop by tablespoon into boiling stock or gravy. Cover and cook 5 minutes.

ISANTI COUNTY had an early logging boom because its forests along the Rum river were near the sawmills of the growing Twin Cities. Logging brought New Englanders, who named their towns Cambridge, Athens, Oxford and Stanford. Many Swedes followed the lumbermen into the area; they thought the climate and scenery much like home.

Hungarian Butter Roll

2 cakes compressed yeast
1 tablespoon sugar
¼ cup scalded milk (lukewarm)
1½ cups flour
½ cup butter
3 egg yolks
1 teaspoon vanilla

Mix flour and shortening as for pie. Dissolve yeast and sugar in milk. Add yeast mixture to egg yolks and vanilla. Beat thoroughly. Add small amount at a time to flour mixture. Place in a clean cloth and set in a bowl of water (cold but not icy) and let remain in water for 45 minutes.

Mix ½ cup sugar and ¼ cup chopped walnuts. Place in shallow pan and take about a teaspoonful of the dough and roll in this mixture; twist twice. Let rise 15 to 20 minutes. Bake in 350 degree oven.

Curry Cheese Sauce for Wild Rice or Game

2 tablespoons fat
1 onion, chopped fine
1 green pepper, chopped fine
½ teaspoon salt
½ teaspoon pepper
1 good pinch allspice
Pinch mace
½ teaspoon curry powder
1 cup processed American cheese
⅔ cup milk

Melt fat; brown onion and pepper. Add cheese (use very low heat). Remove from heat, blend in flour, add spices. Slowly add milk, cook until thick (about 15 minutes). Let stand. About ½ hour before serving, add cream and cook slowly. Amount of cream is a matter of how thick or thin a sauce is desired. This makes about 1 cup.

Almond Kringles

1 cup flour
½ cup butter
1 tablespoon water
1 cup water
½ cup butter
1 cup flour
3 eggs
1 tablespoon almond extract

Mix flour, butter, and tablespoon of water like pie crust. Pat into 2 strips 3″ wide on cookie sheet.

Heat to boiling the cup of water, butter. Remove from heat and add flour. Stir until smooth, then add eggs, 1 at a time, beating until smooth after each addition. Add extract. Spread over pastry and bake 45 minutes at 400 degrees. When cool, frost with powdered sugar icing.

Caramel Dumplings

1½ cups brown sugar
2 cups water
2 tablespoons butter
½ cup sugar
2 tablespoons butter
1½ cups pastry flour
2 teaspoons baking powder
½ cup milk

Mix brown sugar, water, and butter; bring to boil in top of double boiler. Cream butter and sugar; sift flour and baking powder and add alternately with milk. Drop dumplings in syrup and cook them until done. Serve warm with cream.

Mashed Potato Donuts

2 eggs, beaten
1 cup sugar
2 tablespoons salad oil or melted shortening
1 cup mashed potatoes (just as left over)
1 cup sour milk
4½ cups sifted flour
1 teaspoon salt
4 teaspoons baking powder
1 teaspoon nutmeg
1 teaspoon soda

Mix in order given; chill well and roll ½″ thick. Fry in deep fat.

ITASCA COUNTY was often an Indian battle ground and that's the reason for the turtle and snake mounds in Chippewa national forest. The Sioux defeated the Chippewa and built the big turtle mound, pointing north. But the Chippewa came back, massacred every Sioux, and built the coiled snake around the turtle, pointing south as a warning.

Duck with Wild Rice Stuffing

4 small ducks
½ cup wild rice
6 strips bacon
2 stalks celery

1 medium-sized onion
½ green pepper
¼ teaspoon oregano
¼ teaspoon pepper
Salt to taste

Wash the rice well, using several waters, and boil in salted water until tender and fluffy. Sauté the diced bacon until crisp. Add the minced vegetables, onion, celery, and green pepper, and cook until tender but not brown. Combine with the well-drained rice and add the seasonings. Fill the cavities of the ducks with the stuffing and close the openings with small skewers.

Bake in a 325 degree oven about 3 hours. If the ducks are preferred crisp, turn the oven heat to 400 for the last 20-30 minutes of cooking. Place strips of bacon or salt pork over the breasts of the birds if they are not fat enough.

Beer Batter for Fish

¼ cup cornstarch
¼ cup flour
¼ cup beer
2 egg whites, whipped until very stiff
6 walleye fillets

Sift together the cornstarch and flour. Add the beer and mix until the batter is smooth. Fold in the egg whites that have been whipped stiff. Season the fish fillets well and dip in batter. Fry in about 1″ of hot fat until the fillets are well-browned on both sides and the fish is done.

Wild Rice and Pork Chops

1 cup wild rice
8 slices lean bacon
1 medium-sized onion
1 teaspoon salt
¼ teaspoon pepper
½ teaspoon crushed oregano
6 pork chops cut 1½" thick

Wash the wild rice well. Cover generously with hot water and allow to boil about 5 minutes. Drain and rinse with hot water. Cover again with hot water. Add salt. Bring to a boil and cook about 20 minutes, or until the rice is tender. Stir gently with a fork a few times during the cooking process. Drain well.

Dice the bacon and sauté with the minced onion until the bacon is crisp and the onion tender. Add the rice and seasonings and toss to blend well. Place the mixture in a large covered baking dish. Brown the chops well on both sides, sprinkle with salt, pepper, and a little poultry seasoning if desired. Place over the rice. Cover and set the casserole in a pan of water. Bake in a 325 degree oven about 1½ hours, or until the chops are tender.

Make a gravy in the pan in which the pork chops were browned. Add 1 4-ounce can of mushroom slices, with the liquid. The chops will be like individual roasts.

Christmas Tart (Finnish Joulutortut)

3 cups heavy cream, whipped
1 teaspoon baking powder
6½ cups flour
Butter

Whip the cream and add the baking powder and flour that have been sifted together. Weigh the dough and use ½ as much butter as the dough weighs. Soften the butter and work it into the dough. Chill. Roll out small amounts at a time to about ¼" thickness. Cut in squares. From each corner of the square, cut almost to the center. Place a spoon of filling in the center and bring every point to the center to form pinwheel. Press down firmly. Brush tops with slightly-beaten egg and bake in a 425 degree oven about 15 minutes.

Filling
1½ cups cooked prunes
½ cup sugar

Pit prunes and cut in small pieces. Add sugar and stir to blend well. Use for tart filling.

Ice Box Cookies

1 cup brown sugar
1 cup white sugar
1 cup shortening (part butter)
2 eggs
½ teaspoon salt
1 teaspoon soda
1 teaspoon baking powder
4 cups flour
1 teaspoon vanilla
1 cup nut meats, chopped

Sift flour once, measure, and add salt, soda, baking powder and sift again. Cream sugar and shortening; add eggs and vanilla. Add flour mixture, nut meats. Mix thoroughly. Form into 2 rolls and freeze. Cut into thin slices while still frozen and bake until brown at 350 degrees.

Caramel Pecan Pie

Make a graham cracker crust by combining 1½ cups fine graham cracker crumbs, ⅓ cup melted butter, and ¼ cup sugar. Press into buttered 9″ pie plate; chill until firm, about 45 minutes.

Caramel Filling

1 envelope unflavored gelatin
¼ cup cold water
½ pound (28) vanilla caramels
¾ cup milk
Dash salt
1 cup cream, whipped
½ cup pecans, chopped
1 teaspoon vanilla

Soften gelatin in cold water. Melt caramels in milk in top of double boiler. Add softened gelatin and salt, stirring to dissolve. Chill until slightly set. Fold in whipped cream, chopped pecans, and vanilla. Fill crust. Trim with pecan halves. Chill 2 to 3 hours.

Grandmother's Chocolate Chip Crumb Cookies

⅓ cup butter
1½ cups flour
½ cup brown sugar
¼ teaspoon salt
1 teaspoon baking powder
2 egg yolks

Beat egg yolks, add sugar, and shortening, then beat again; add flour, salt, and baking powder. Press this crumbly mixture into a 7" x 11" pan. Cover with topping and bake at 325 degrees for 25 to 30 minutes.

Topping

2 egg whites
1 cup brown sugar
1 package chocolate chips
½ cup broken nut meats
1 teaspoon vanilla

Beat egg whites until very stiff, add brown sugar and mix well. Add remaining ingredients.

Raised Donuts

2 packages dry yeast
¼ cup warm water (115 degrees)
¼ cup sugar
½ teaspoon mace
½ teaspoon nutmeg
2 cups sifted flour
3 tablespoons dry milk
1 cup warm water (115 degrees)
⅓ cup shortening
2 eggs
2 cups flour
1 teaspoon salt

Sprinkle yeast over ¼ cup water. Sift all dry ingredients together, including dry milk; add 1 cup water. Stir the yeast mixture, add to flour mixture and beat until well blended. Mix in shortening and eggs. Lastly sift the 2 cups of flour and salt together and add. Let rest 10 minutes. Knead, let rise until double. Roll out and cut with large doughnut cutter. Let rise until double and fry in deep fat at 365 degrees. Glaze with a mixture of 1 cup powdered sugar, ¼ cup boiling water, and vanilla.

KANABEC COUNTY'S name is Chippewa for Snake, the area's principal river and a center of logging activities. At Mora, a museum houses a complete set of early lumbering tools and equipment. Near Mora is Knife lake, so named because there the explorer, Radisson, gave to the Indians the first steel knives they had seen.

Swedish Torte

½ cup granulated sugar
4 tablespoons sweet milk
1 cup pastry flour
½ teaspoon almond flavoring
Dash salt
2 tablespoons butter
2 egg yolks
1 teaspoon baking powder
½ teaspoon lemon flavoring

Cream butter and sugar; add egg yolks, beaten lightly. Sift dry ingredients, add alternately with milk. Put into buttered layer pans and top with nut meringue.

Nut Meringue

4 egg whites
⅛ teaspoon cream of tartar
Almond flavoring
1 cup granulated sugar
⅛ teaspoon salt
½ cup chopped nuts

Add salt, cream of tartar to the egg whites and beat. Gradually add the sugar and flavoring and beat until smooth. Heap this meringue on the uncooked layers; sprinkle the chopped nuts over the meringue and bake in moderate oven (350 degrees) about 45 minutes or until a nice golden brown. Let cool in tins. When ready to serve put layers together with the following custard.

Custard

1 cup milk
2 egg yolks
1 teaspoon vanilla
3 tablespoons sugar
1 heaping teaspoon cornstarch
Dash salt

Cook in double boiler and let cool. Put between layers. Top Swedish Torte with whipped cream, sweetened and flavored.

Sandbakelse (Scandinavian cookie)

½ pound butter (1 cup)
1 cup sugar
1 egg
3 cups flour

Cream butter well, add sugar and cream until smooth. Add egg and beat well. Add flour and stir until smooth. Flavor with crushed cardamom seed. Press into sandbakelse tins and bake in a moderate oven (350 degrees) until slightly browned.

Fattigman (Scandinavian cookie)

Beat 4 egg yolks and 2 whites slightly, add 6 tablespoons cream, 7 tablespoons sugar and beat again. Add 3 tablespoons whiskey and beat. Add 3 cups flour. Chill, then roll out very thin and cut in triangle shapes with a small cutter and fry in deep fat for about 2 or 3 minutes until brown. Drain on paper. Makes about 70 to 80 thin wafers.

Ham Balls (Swedish)

1 pound ground smoked ham
1½ pounds ground pork
2 cups bread crumbs
2 eggs, well beaten
1 teaspoon dry mustard
1 cup milk
1½ cups brown sugar
½ cup water
½ cup vinegar

Combine brown sugar, vinegar, water, and mustard. Stir until sugar is dissolved. Combine meats, crumbs, eggs, and milk. Mix thoroughly. Form in small balls. Place in casserole. Pour brown sugar mixture over meat balls. Bake in slow oven (270 degrees) for 1¼ hours. Baste frequently with sauce.

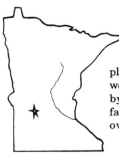

KANDIYOHI COUNTY'S prairies were part of the area plundered by the angry Sioux in 1862. Thirteen settlers were murdered at Willmar. Their neighbors were saved by a freak accident. Trembling in the dirt cellar, the family heard the Indians crash into a trunk, which fell over the trap door, hiding it and saving the family.

Berliner Kranser (Scandinavian cookie)

4 egg yolks
1 cup sugar
6 cups flour
1¾ cups butter
Yolks of 3 hard-boiled eggs

Beat the 4 egg yolks thoroughly and add the sugar. Rub the hard-boiled yolks until smooth, and add to the sugar and yolk mixture. Blend the butter and flour until very crumbly and add to the above mixture, and mix thoroughly. Form into loaf and chill. Cut off little pieces and roll about the thickness of a pencil and 5" long. Form into wreaths. Dip into slightly-beaten egg whites and then into crushed loaf sugar or chopped almonds. Bake in medium oven (350 degrees) until brown.

Apple Nut Pudding

2 eggs
1 cup sugar
¾ cup flour
¾ teaspoon salt
1 teaspoon baking powder
½ teaspoon cinnamon
¼ teaspoon nutmeg
1 teaspoon almond extract
¾ cup nutmeats, chopped
1½ cups raw apples, diced

Beat eggs until fluffy. Add sugar gradually, beating after each addition. Sift together flour, salt, baking powder, cinnamon, and diced apples. Mix thoroughly. Bake at 325 degrees for 50 minutes in 8" x 8" pan.

Grandmother Negaard's Meat Balls

3 pounds ground round steak
(ground at least 4 times)
½ teaspoon ginger
¼ teaspoon nutmeg
¼ teaspoon pepper
1 quart heavy cream

Add spices to meat, then blend in cream. Beat until light. Work and work and work the meat mixture until light. Form into small balls. Brown in butter. Make a gravy from fryings in pan; add small amount of flour and water. Pour gravy over meat balls. Heat thoroughly and serve.

"Floating Islands" Dessert

1 quart rich milk
3 eggs, separated
½ cup sugar
¼ cup sugar

Pour the milk into a saucepan. Heat slowly. Beat the egg yolks well. Add the ½ cup sugar and continue beating until mixture is fluffy. Pour egg mixture slowly into heated milk, stirring constantly. Cook over low heat until thickened, then pour into a serving bowl. Beat the egg whites until frothy. Add ¼ cup sugar and beat until mixture forms into peaks. Spoon the egg whites onto the first mixture, keeping each spoonful separated (these are the "islands"). In the center of each island, place a teaspoon of apple jelly.

Osta Kaka (Swedish dessert)

1 gallon milk
½ rennet tablet
1 cup cream
1 cup flour
2 eggs
½ cup sugar

Stir a cup of milk slowly into the cup of flour. Add it to a gallon of lukewarm milk. Add rennet tablet that has been dissolved in a little warm water. Stir well for just a few seconds. Let set 1 hour or until mixture is very firm. Cut with knife. Drain off all the whey. Add cream, well-beaten eggs, and sugar and stir well. Bake in a casserole at 300 degrees for 2 hours. It is done when well browned. Serve with cranberry relish or cranberry jelly.

KITTSON COUNTY was named for an American Fur Company agent at Pembina, who first made use of trains of oxcarts to carry furs to markets. Its county seat, Hallock, is named for a journalist and sportsman who built, in the raw new town, a swank hotel with running water on every floor, bathrooms, speaking tubes, and kennel and gun rooms.

Rice Pudding (Swedish)

    1 quart milk
    ½ cup rice
    ¼ cup sugar
    2 tablespoons butter
    ¼ teaspoon salt
    2 eggs
    ½ cup raisins
    ⅛ teaspoon nutmeg

Pour boiling water over raisins and let stand a few minutes. Place 3 cups milk, sugar, and salt in top of double boiler. Wash the rice and add to the milk and sugar; cook 1½ hours.

Beat the eggs well and add to the remaining cup of milk. Mix into the rice. Now pour into a greased baking dish, dot butter over the top. Sprinkle with nutmeg.

Place the baking dish in a pan of hot water and bake at 350 degrees for 1 hour.

Flat Bread

    1¼ cups white flour
    ¼ teaspoon salt
    ¼ teaspoon soda
    2 tablespoons sugar
    ⅓ cup graham flour
    ⅛ cup lard
    ¼ cup cream
    ¼ cup buttermilk

Sift white flour, salt, soda, and sugar together 3 times. Add graham flour and cut in lard as for pie crust. Add cream and buttermilk.

Divide dough into 6 or 8 parts and let rest 15 minutes. Now roll out very thin on floured board. Prick with a fork. Bake at 350 degrees for about 15 minutes.

Filled Chocolate Cupcakes

1½ cups cake flour
¾ cup sugar
1 teaspoon soda
½ teaspoon salt
1½ squares chocolate, melted
1 heaping tablespoon butter, melted
1 cup buttermilk
Whipped cream

Mix ingredients in order given, melting chocolate and butter together. Bake in cupcake cases at 350 degrees.

When cool, cut cap off top and save, scoop out center of cupcake to within ½″ of bottom and sides. Fill hole in cupcake with whipped cream. Put cap back on and ice with chocolate icing.

Chocolate Icing

1 cup liquid, half milk and half cream
1½ squares chocolate
2 cups sugar

Boil milk, cream, and chocolate until thick (like chocolate pudding). Add sugar, boil slowly to soft ball stage (this is about 242 degrees on a candy thermometer). Cool. Then beat with electric beater, adding a small amount of cream to make the right consistency.

Cinnamon Apple Puffs

1 cup sugar
1 cup water
½ teaspoon red food coloring
1½ pounds tart apples (4 to 5 apples),
    peeled and thinly sliced
1½ cups sifted flour
½ teaspoon salt
2 teaspoons baking powder
¼ cup shortening
¾ cup milk

Boil sugar, water, and food coloring until syrupy (about 5 minutes). Place apples in a greased shallow 8″ x 12″ baking dish. Pour syrup over apples.

Sift flour, salt, and baking powder together; cut in shortening with pastry blender, and then add milk to make a soft dough. Drop 12 spoonfuls of dough on top of apples and make a dent in top of each. Place in the dents a mixture of 2 tablespoons melted butter, 2 tablespoons sugar, and ½ teaspoon cinnamon. Bake 25 to 30 minutes at 450 degrees. Serve warm, with cream, if desired. Serves 8 to 10.

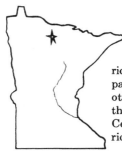

KOOCHICHING COUNTY includes Nett lake, where wild rice grows profusely. To gather it, Chippewa Indians paddle into the swamp. While one guides the canoe, the other threshes the rice heads with two sticks. On shore, the grain is roasted, then stamped on to beat off the hulls. Ceremonial dances still accompany the harvest of the rice, long an Indian food staple.

Minestrone Soup (Italian)

    1 **pound fresh peas**
    1 **cup celery, diced**
    2 **carrots, diced**
    1 **large-sized onion, sliced**
    1 **cup canned tomatoes**
    ½ **cup olive oil**
    ¾ **pound Vermicelli (fine spaghetti)**
    3 **quarts water**
    3 **potatoes, diced**
    ⅛ **teaspoon salt**
    Dash pepper
    Parmesan cheese, grated

Clean all vegetables. Saute onions and potatoes in hot oil about 10 minutes or until medium brown. Add tomatoes, salt, and pepper; cover; cook slowly about 15 minutes.

In a separate pot, bring 3 quarts of water to boil. Add celery, peas, and carrots; cover; cook 15 minutes or until vegetables are tender. Add all other ingredients and the Vermicelli broken into 1" pieces. Cover and cook 20 minutes. Serve very hot with grated Parmesan cheese. Serves 6 to 8.

Red Flannel Hash

    3 **tablespoons drippings**
    1½ **cups cooked beef, chopped**
    2 **tablespoons cream**
    4 **cups cooked potatoes, chopped**
    1½ **cups cooked beets, chopped**
    ¾ **cup onion, chopped**

Heat drippings in frying pan. Combine remaining ingredients and blend. Spread mixture evenly over bottom of pan. Brown slowly until a crust forms on the bottom. Turn as an omelet. Serves 6.

Old-fashioned Sour Cream Cookies

1 cup sour cream
¾ cup shortening
3 eggs
2 cups sugar
1 teaspoon soda
1 teaspoon baking powder
1 teaspoon lemon extract
1 teaspoon vanilla
Flour enough to make a stiff dough

Roll out and sprinkle sugar on top. Bake until a light tan in a moderate oven (350 degrees). These are thick, soft cookies.

Applesauce Nut Bread

2 cups flour
¾ cup sugar
3 teaspoons baking powder
1 teaspoon salt
½ teaspoon soda
1 teaspoon cinnamon
½ cup walnuts, chopped
1 egg, beaten
1 cup applesauce
2 tablespoons shortening, melted

Sift dry ingredients together. Stir in egg, applesauce, shortening, and nuts. Bake 1 hour at 350 degrees.

Civil War Cookies

3 cups sugar
2 cups thick sour cream
1 cup butter
3 eggs
1 teaspoon ginger
2 teaspoons soda
Flour to mix smooth

Roll out thin, cut, and sprinkle with sugar. Bake at 350 degrees until brown.

LAC QUI PARLE COUNTY takes its name from the lake, a French translation of the Indian name for "Lake That Speaks." It was in this county that the 1862 Indian massacre came to an end. The Sioux turned over to General Sibley 269 white prisoners from the Minnesota river valley. The site later became the first unit in the state park system.

Egg and Vegetable Casserole

2 cups cooked potatoes, diced
1 cup celery, diced
6 hard-cooked eggs, sliced
Chopped onions, about 2 tablespoons
2 cups medium white sauce

Add all the ingredients above to the cooked white sauce. Pour into well-greased casserole dish and top with ½ cup of grated cheese. Bake in hot oven (425 degrees) about 15 minutes or until brown. Serves 6. A little chopped pimiento may be added to this casserole, if preferred.

Medium White Sauce

4 tablespoons fat
4 tablespoons flour
½ teaspoon salt
Dash pepper
2 cups milk

Melt the fat in top of a double boiler. Add the flour, salt, and pepper. Blend thoroughly. Pour in the cold milk and stir constantly until thick. Cook about 10 minutes.

Never-fail Angel Food Doughnuts

3 eggs, beaten light
1 cup sugar
1 cup sour cream
1 cup sour milk
1 level teaspoon soda
½ teaspoon ginger
½ teaspoon nutmeg
1 teaspoon salt
2 rounded teaspoons baking powder
5 cups flour

Beat eggs, sugar, cream, and milk. Add sifted dry ingredients. Roll and cut. Let doughnuts rest 20 minutes or longer before frying. Fry in deep fat.

85

Prize White Bread

At the urging of my family I entered a loaf of bread in State Fair competition. When it received Sweepstakes two years in succession, there were many requests for the recipe. By using good ingredients and accurate measurements, good results are assured. Mrs. F. L. Hansberger, Dawson.

2 teaspoons sugar
½ cup lukewarm water
2 cakes compressed yeast
4 cups lukewarm water
½ cup white sugar
6 cups enriched white flour
¾ to 1 cup dry milk
2 tablespoons salt
¼ cup soft shortening, lard or butter
5½ cups (about) enriched white flour

Mix first 3 ingredients and let stand 10 minutes. Add the next 4 ingredients and beat with electric mixer. Add salt, soft shortening, and final amount of flour. Mix together into a ball. Turn out on floured board, cover with greased bowl and let rest 15 to 20 minutes.

Knead well, adding just enough more flour to keep from sticking. Let rise until fully doubled. Punch down, let rise again until nearly double. Divide into 4 balls. Let rest 10 minutes. Shape into loaves. When doubled in size, bake at 350 degrees for 50 minutes. Grease loaves as soon as taken from oven. Leave uncovered until cool.

Ginger Bread Cake

1½ cups white sugar
¾ cup lard
2 eggs, beaten
1 cup molasses
1 cup boiling water
1 teaspoon soda, dissolved in
   boiling water
1 teaspoon cinnamon
½ teaspoon ginger
¼ teaspoon cloves
½ teaspoon salt
2½ cups flour
1 cup raisins, ground

Bake for 1 hour at 350 degrees. The older this cake gets, the better it tastes. It does not dry out.

LAKE COUNTY draws tourists by the thousands to some of the state's most famous sights. There's Split Rock lighthouse on Lake Superior, perched higher than any other lighthouse in the nation. There are breathtaking waterfalls on the Gooseberry, Baptism and Manitou rivers. And there's the sheer precipice of Silver Creek Cliff and its unsurpassed view of Lake Superior.

Dark Fruit Cake

3 cups brown sugar
2 cups butter
6 eggs
1 pound raisins
1 pound currants
1 pound mixed fruit
1 pound red and green cherries
1 cup walnuts (or more)
1 cup almonds (or more)
½ cup molasses
½ cup sour milk
4 cups flour
1 tablespoon cinnamon
1 teaspoon mace
1 teaspoon cloves
1 teaspoon nutmeg
1 teaspoon soda

Cream the butter and sugar and add the spices. Mix well and add the molasses and sour milk. Add the beaten yolks of eggs and mix well. Add the 4 cups of flour alternately with the beaten whites of eggs. Dissolve the soda in a little warm water and stir into the mixture thoroughly.

Mix the fruit and nuts together and stir in 2 tablespoons of flour. Add to cake mixture and mix all well.

Place in baking loaf pans lined with waxed paper, buttered. Bake in moderate oven (275-300 degrees) for 2 hours. Allow to cool in pans.

More fruit and nuts may be added if desired. This recipe makes 2 large loaf cakes or 9 small ones.

Poppy Seed Cake

        1 cup poppy seed
        ¾ cup scalded milk
        1½ cups sugar
        ¾ cup butter
        ¾ cup cold milk
        3 teaspoons baking powder
        3 cups flour
        4 egg whites, beaten

Soak poppy seed in scalded milk overnight.

Cream butter and sugar well, add dry ingredients (sifted together 3 times) alternately with milk, fold in poppy seed mixture and lastly the egg whites.

Bake in 3 layers in 9″ pans at 350 degrees for 25 to 30 minutes. Cool. Put filling between layers; frost with white icing and sprinkle with nuts.

        Filling

        Juice of 1 lemon
        1 cup sugar
        2 tablespoons cornstarch
        1 cup scalding water
        1 pinch salt

Cook until thick.

Almond Pear Delights

This is a Greek recipe which was developed by a leading home economist and food consultant in Greece. Mrs. M. Albert Henry, Two Harbors.

        1½ pounds almonds, blanched, ground fine
        1½ cups sugar
        ½ cup Farina
        1½ cups rose water
        4 cups powdered sugar, sifted
        Whole cloves

Let blanched almonds dry for a few hours, then grind. (An electric blender whirs them fine in split seconds.) Add sugar and Farina. Add to the mixture 6 to 8 tablespoons of rose water, enough to make a soft dough. Shape balls of the dough into small pears, placing a clove in the top of each for stem. Line up the pears on a greased, lightly-floured cookie sheet and bake at 300 degrees for 20 minutes or until browned lightly. Dip pears while hot into rose water, then into powdered sugar. Let cool for a few minutes, then re-dip in the sugar.

LAKE OF THE WOODS COUNTY lies along the Canadian border and its namesake lake and includes the Northwest Angle, the northernmost point of land in the nation. It was there that La Verendrye built Fort St. Charles in 1732. From it sped the voyageurs in their plumed caps and gaudy sashes, with their ballads and renowned skill with canoes.

Apple Gravy

  1 can sliced apples
  1 tablespoon butter
  1 tablespoon flour
  1 cup thin white sauce
  1 teaspoon lemon peel, grated
  ½ cup sour cream

Saute sliced apples in the butter until hot. Dust with flour and brown to a delicate golden color. Stir in white sauce and lemon rind. Bring to a boil. Remove from heat and stir in sour cream. This is delicious served with roast pork, boiled beef, or tongue.

Broiled Lake Trout

Wash fish in salt and vinegar water (3 tablespoons vinegar, 1 tablespoon salt in 1 quart water.)

Dry and split in half. Season with salt and pepper. Place skin side down on shallow baking dish. Pour 1 cup heavy cream over fish or use ¼ cup softened butter spread over fish. Broil 20 to 25 minutes, 6" from broiler. Do not turn.

Corn and Dried Beef Hot Dish

  1 8-ounce package narrow egg
    noodles (cooked)
  ½ pound dried beef, cut up
  2 onions, chopped
  1 small green pepper, diced
  1 No. 2 can whole kernel corn
  2 cans mushroom soup
  2 tablespoons beefsteak sauce
  2 tablespoons butter

Brown dried beef slightly in the butter. Add onion and continue browning a little more. Add rest of ingredients and bake in casserole 30 to 35 minutes in moderate oven (375 degrees).

Walleyed Pike Salad or Appetizer

          3 or 4 walleye fillets
          1 can shoestring beets, drained
          1 can ripe olives, chopped
          1 can green olives, chopped
          1 can mushrooms
          ¾ pound sharp cheese, cubed
          ¾ pound salami, cut up
          4 ripe tomatoes, diced
          1 onion, chopped fine
          1 can tomato sauce
          Dash garlic salt
          French dressing to taste

Steam, then cool and crumble fillets. Add remaining ingredients. Allow to set at least 3 hours or longer in refrigerator. Serve on lettuce as salad or use as appetizer.

Baked Wild Duck

Dress as any poultry. Wipe inside and outside with a damp cloth. Place 1 unpeeled orange and 1 unpeeled but cored apple in the inside of duck. (Gash the orange ½" deep in the form of a cross.) Tie legs to tail. Place the duck in a very hot oven (500 degrees) for 30 minutes. Then remove from oven, take out fruit and pour off excess fat.

When cool fill with Lake of the Woods Wild Rice Stuffing and sew skin together. Dredge with ½ cup flour to which ½ teaspoon salt has been added. Place in a quick oven (450 degrees) for 30 minutes until the flour is browned, then reduce heat to slow oven (300 degrees) and finish baking, allowing 25 minutes to each pound. Baste every 10 minutes of the last half hour with 1 cup lukewarm water.

By cooking wild duck in this manner, disagreeable or strong fat is removed.

Lake of the Woods Wild Rice Stuffing

          1 cup wild rice
          3 teaspoons salt
          ½ teaspoon pepper
          1 cup celery, diced
          Parsley

Cook clean wild rice in 4 cups boiling, salted water; drain. Add remaining ingredients. When cold, use as stuffing for wild duck, goose.

LE SUEUR COUNTY named for the French explorer who was first to travel the Minnesota river, later became famous for the quality limestone quarried around Kasota. At first, the limestone was used in heavy construction. Jim Hill's beautiful stone arch bridge in Minneapolis is a striking example. Later, after concrete's arrival, Kasota stone was used as trim.

Steamed Cranberry Pudding

    1½ cups flour
    1 teaspoon baking powder
    ¼ teaspoon salt
    ½ cup molasses
    ⅓ cup warm water (can use hot water and
        melt shortening in it)
    2 tablespoons shortening, melted
    2 teaspoons soda
    ⅔ cup canned cranberry sauce, drained

Sift first 3 ingredients together; mix molasses, water, shortening, and soda together. Combine and fold in cranberry sauce.

Pour into greased lidded mold and steam 1 hour plus 15 minutes. (Put waxed paper between the dough and the lid of the mold. The container holding the water should also be covered with a lid. The water should surround the pudding mold about ¾ of the way up the side of the mold.)

Unmold pudding and serve with sauce.

    Sauce
    1 cup sugar
    ½ cup cream
    ¼ cup butter
    1 teaspoon vanilla

Heat sugar and cream (don't boil); remove from heat and add butter in small chunks so that they melt. Add vanilla.

Baked-on Frosting

    5 tablespoons brown sugar
    3 tablespoons butter
    2 tablespoons cream (sweet or sour)
    ½ cup coconut, grated

Melt brown sugar, butter, and cream. Add grated coconut. When cake is done, spread the above evenly over top of cake. Put under broiler until it bubbles and is slightly brown.

Vomachka

Minnesota's bountiful supply of game and fish has provided our family with many excellent meals year after year. We have enjoyed deer, bear, raccoon, jackrabbit, cottontail, squirrel, turtle, frogs, wild ducks, grouse, pheasants, crow, blackbird, grackle and every species of edible fish that our lakes and rivers produce.

Of all these, a top favorite would be the Booya or "Vomachka," as we Bohemians call it, made from the gizzards and hearts of ducks.— Mrs. B. A. Ebert, LeCenter

Take gizzards and hearts from 8 or 10 wild ducks. Or, you may use a pork or veal heart to extend a small amount of game. Cook with 4 cups of water, 2 bay leaves, 4 whole allspice, and 1 teaspoon of salt. Cook 30 minutes in pressure sauce pan at 10 pounds, or cook in open kettle until tender.

Prepare 3 medium carrots, 3 stalks celery, 2 medium onions, 2 sprigs parsley, and ½ teaspoon salt. When meat is cooked, cut it into bite-sized pieces and return to broth with vegetables and cook until vegetables are almost tender. At that time add 1 cup of rich sour cream to which ¼ cup of flour has been added; cook until vegetables are tender and Vomachka is thickened. Add dash of pepper and monosodium glutamate.

It should be the consistency of a heavy cream soup. If water has evaporated in the cooking, you may need to add a little. Cream may be soured by the addition of vinegar or lemon juice, and some folks may prefer to add a bit more vinegar at the time of eating. Serve in bowls with dry rye or white bread or over boiled potatoes, either mashed or chopped coarsely.

Honey Bread

This is a French recipe which Sister Ella Ness, a missionary to Madagascar, brought back to Minnesota. Wives of the French officials used to serve this bread when they entertained the missionaries. Miss Alice Ponwith, Cleveland.

> 1 cup honey
> 1 cup milk
> ½ cup sugar
> 2 egg yolks
> 2¼ cups flour
> 1 teaspoon soda
> ½ teaspoon salt

Heat slowly honey, milk, and sugar until dissolved. Cool. Beat egg yolks slightly and add. Sift dry ingredients together and stir in. Pour into large loaf pan which has been lined with paper and greased. Bake at 350 degrees until wooden pick thrust into center comes out clean—about 75-80 minutes.

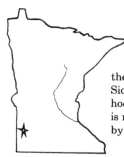

LINCOLN COUNTY has a lake called Stay, named for the French-Canadian trapper, Frank Stay, who fought the Sioux in 1862 from a trench he'd scraped out with a garden hoe. Someone later recorded his comment: "By gor! I is no thief, but I steal a hoe once from the Indians, and, by gor! That hoe save my life!"

Beef Pinwheels

>   1 pound hamburger
>   1½ teaspoons salt
>   ⅛ teaspoon pepper
>   2 tablespoons melted butter
>   ½ cup soft bread crumbs
>   2 tablespoons tomato juice or milk
>   1½ cups seasoned mashed potatoes
>   1½ cups seasoned mashed peas

Mix together all ingredients except potatoes and peas. Place between 2 sheets of waxed paper. Use rolling pin to roll into a rectangle about ⅛" to ½" thick. Remove top waxed paper. Spread mashed potatoes on half of meat and peas on remaining half. Roll meat firmly, jelly roll fashion, starting with the end of the rectangle covered with the peas. Wrap in waxed paper and chill in refrigerator. Cut into 1" slices and either broil for 10 minutes, or bake for 20 minutes at 375 degrees, after brushing slices with melted butter.

Beef Bordeaux

>   2½ pounds beef round
>   1 cup coarsely sliced celery, green
>   peppers, onion, and mushrooms combined
>   1½ teaspoons paprika
>   ½ teaspoon garlic powder
>   3 cups beef broth
>   1 bay leaf

Cut meat into cubes, string on skewers. Dredge in flour mixed with salt, pepper, garlic powder, and paprika. Brown well in a little hot lard. When meat is brown, place in shallow pan, put vegetables over and cover with broth. Place in a 400 degree oven. When ingredients begin to bubble, reduce heat to 325 degrees and cook until tender. If stock thickens too much, add more broth or water. Serves 6.

Babe in Blanket (Polish Christmas cookie)

1 cup butter
1 cup sour cream
2 egg yolks
4 cups flour
1 teaspoon salt
1 teaspoon cinnamon
2 tablespoons lemon juice

Sift flour, salt, and cinnamon. Cut in shortening with pastry blender. Add cream, yolks, and lemon juice. Chill dough overnight. The next day, make the meringue. Roll out the chilled dough on board dusted with confectioner's sugar. Roll it paper thin and cut into 3" squares. Put about 1 teaspoon of meringue filling on each square. Fold 2 opposite corners over each other. Place on greased cookie sheet. Bake at 350 degrees for 25 minutes.

Meringue

2 egg whites, beaten stiff but not dry
½ cup sugar
½ pound walnuts, ground
2½ teaspoons cinnamon
⅛ teaspoon salt

Add sugar gradually to stiffly-beaten egg whites; beat until meringue forms stiff peaks. Fold in remaining ingredients.

Bishop's Bread

3 cups flour
2 teaspoons baking powder
½ teaspoon soda
1 teaspoon salt
1¼ teaspoons cinnamon
9 tablespoons fat
1 cup sour milk
1 cup brown sugar
2 eggs, well beaten

Cream fat, add brown sugar gradually and cream until fluffy. Add well-beaten eggs. Add sifted dry ingredients alternately with sour milk. Cover with topping. Bake at 350 degrees for 35 to 40 minutes. Use one 13" x 9½" pan or two 8" x 8" pans.

Topping

½ cup brown sugar
2 tablespoons butter
¼ teaspoon cinnamon
2 tablespoons flour

Combine all ingredients.

LYON COUNTY'S seat, Marshall, tells the railroad story. The town had two sod huts before the railroad came. The railroad arrived October 12, 1872, and within a year Marshall boomed with a blacksmith shop, a brick kiln, telegraph office, lumberyard, millinery, photographer, and all the trappings of a frontier town.

Poor Man's Pea Soup

This "receipt" was an old family recipe when mother was born in 1868; it's precious to me because of its memories. When I was a child, my younger sister and brother and I would gather around mother during the cold winter evenings, begging her to tell us stories.

Our favorite story was of her early childhood in the hills near Winona: One year the crops had been poor and the snowfall seemingly endless. There were rumors of dreadful starvation and illness in the Indian settlement.

One evening grandfather came home with what looked like a bundle of rags but proved to be an Indian. The children huddled under the bed for safety. Grandfather told his wife to feed the man so grandmother filled a huge bowl with the pea soup simmering on the stove.

From that time on, they became accustomed to seeing an Indian loitering around the barn, and grandfather would always invite him in. Food was not plentiful, but grandmother kept the pea soup handy. When spring came, they never saw an Indian on the place again but often a basket made of willow twigs with the first lush berries of the season or brook trout or game would be left on their doorstep. Mrs. Eleanor Lutz, Marshall.

> 2 cups split yellow peas
> Soda, pinch
> Salt to taste
> 2 bay leaves
> Allspice
> 1 cup raw potatoes, diced
> ½ cup onions, chopped
> 2 tablespoons butter
> Salt and pepper

Cover peas with water, add pinch of soda and boil for a few minutes. Drain off the water. Cover again with fresh water, add salt to taste, bay leaves, and a few allspice. Cook slowly until peas are soft. Then add potatoes, onions, butter, salt, and pepper. Cook until potatoes are tender. Makes 1 quart of soup. More water may be added in case of "unexpected" company.

Borsch

My grandmother was born on the Black Sea in Russia and came to this country when she was 15. She settled with her family around Mountain Lake. This is one of her recipes which has been handed down from mother to daughter. Mrs. Del Fox, Marshall.

2½ to 3 pounds soup meat
Salt to taste
1 teaspoon dill seeds, or handful fresh dill
1 bay leaf
12 whole black peppers
¾ head cabbage, cut up
1 bunch carrots, diced
Several stalks celery, cut up
¼ green pepper
1 onion, sliced
1 cup tomato juice
½ cup cream

Cook soup meat in ample water and skim as it is cooking. Add salt. Put fresh dill or dill seeds, bay leaf, and black peppers in a bag and add to mixture. When meat is almost tender, add all remaining ingredients except cream and cook until vegetables are tender. Just before serving, add the cream. (Don't boil cream, or it will curdle.) Dill gives the soup a distinctive flavor.

Lincoln-Lee Dumpling Dessert

1 cup brown sugar
2 cups water
½ cup butter
1 cup flour
½ cup sugar
1 teaspoon baking powder
½ teaspoon salt
1 cup raisins
½ cup pecans, chopped
½ cup milk

Boil sugar, water, and butter. Sift the flour, sugar, baking powder, and salt. Add the raisins, pecans, and milk to the sifted dry ingredients. Pour the boiling syrup into 9″ x 9″ x 12″ pan and drop batter into syrup by spoonfuls. Bake for 20 minutes at 500 degrees. Serve warm with whipped cream.

Mc LEOD COUNTY named for a "dignified, eloquent and charming" fur trader, was the scene of one of the brave stands against the warring Sioux in 1862. With many settlements deserted and even Twin Cities people in flight, Hutchinson stood her ground. Men and boys, too old and too young for the Civil War, built a stockade and won their battle.

"Pride of Minnesota" Cookies

1 cup brown sugar
1 cup white sugar
1 cup shortening
2 eggs
1 cup coconut
3 cups quick-rolled oats
2 cups flour
1 teaspoon soda
1 teaspoon baking powder
½ teaspoon salt
1 teaspoon vanilla
1 cup nutmeats

Beat eggs, add sugar, and softened shortening; mix well. Add coconut, nutmeats, and vanilla. Sift and measure the flour and add salt, soda, and baking powder; sift together and add to first mixture.

Add rolled oats and mix thoroughly. Roll into small balls the size of a walnut. Press down on cookie sheet, crease with fork if desired. Bake at 375 degrees 9 minutes or until nicely browned. Crease with fork dipped in water, then sugar if desired.

Frozen Cranberry Salad

1 pound cranberries
2 cups sugar
2 cups water
3 tablespoons lemon juice
½ pint whipping cream
¼ cup powdered sugar
¼ cup mayonnaise
Chopped nuts

Cook cranberries in usual way with sugar and water. Cool. Put in pan 9" x 9" and mush with fork. Add lemon juice. Whip cream, add powdered sugar and mayonnaise, folding carefully. Spread over cranberries and cover with finely-chopped nuts. Freeze. Serve on lettuce.

Stollen (German holiday bread)

1 package active dry yeast or
    1 cake compressed yeast
¼ cup water
½ cup butter or lard
1 cup milk, scalded
¼ cup sugar
1 teaspoon salt
¼ teaspoon ground cardamom
4½ to 5 cups sifted flour
1 egg
1 cup seedless raisins
½ cup currants
½ cup nuts, coarsely chopped

Soften yeast in ¼ cup warm water. Melt butter in hot milk; add sugar, salt, and cardamom; cool to lukewarm. Stir in 2 cups of the flour. Add egg and beat well. Stir in softened yeast, fruit, and nuts. Add remaining flour to make soft dough. Turn out on lightly-floured surface.

Cover and let rest 10 minutes. Knead 5 to 8 minutes until satiny. Place in lightly-greased bowl, turning once to grease surface. Cover; let rise in a warm place until double, about 1½ hours. Punch down; turn out on lightly-floured surface and divide into 3 equal parts. Cover; let rest 10 minutes.

Roll each part into a 12″ by 7″ rectangle. Without stretching dough, fold long side over to within 1″ of opposite side to make typical stollen shape; seal edges. Place on greased baking sheets. Cover and let rise until almost double, about 30 to 40 minutes. Bake in moderate oven (375 degrees) 20 to 25 minutes or until golden brown. Makes 3 loaves.

While warm, brush with icing (2 cups sifted confectioner's sugar, ¼ cup hot water, and 1 teaspoon butter.)

Sour Cream Raisin Pie

Pastry for 2 crusts
1 cup sour cream
⅔ cup sugar
3 eggs
½ cup raisins, chopped
½ teaspoon cloves
1 teaspoon cinnamon

Cook all ingredients together, then cool. Mixture will thicken when it gets cool.

Bake with 2 crusts.

MAHNOMEN COUNTY realized a land boom when the Soo Line opened up the area for settlers just after the turn of the century. But the land belonged to the Indians and could not be sold. The boom came when the Indian Bureau released land for sale. The settlers organized Mahnomen county in 1906; much of it is still the White Earth reservation.

Glazed Orange Nut Drops

1¼ cups flour, sifted
1 cup brown sugar
½ cup butter
¼ cup sour milk
1 egg
½ cup nuts, chopped
1 teaspoon baking powder
¼ teaspoon soda
½ teaspoon salt
1 teaspoon vanilla
1½ teaspoons orange rind, grated

Mix and drop onto greased cookie sheet. Bake at 375 degrees until brown. While warm, dip tops in glaze.

Glaze

1 cup powdered sugar
3 tablespoons orange juice
3 teaspoons orange rind, grated

Hot Chicken Cashew Casserole

1½ cups chicken
1½ cups celery, cut fine
2 tablespoons green pepper, cut fine
2 tablespoons onion, minced
2 tablespoons lemon juice
½ teaspoon salt
Pepper
1 cup cooked macaroni shells
½ cup cashews
¾ cup mayonnaise
1 cup potato chips, crushed

Mix all together and sprinkle potato chips on top. Bake 20 minutes at 450 degrees.

Ricky's Chocolate Sauce

2 squares chocolate
9 tablespoons sugar
6 tablespoons cream
1 egg yolk
1 teaspoon vanilla

Melt chocolate; add sugar and cream in which yolk has been mixed. Bring to a boil and boil 2 to 3 minutes, stirring constantly. Add vanilla. Serves 4. Sauce may be re-warmed by adding a little more cream.

Tangy Crab Rarebit

2 tablespoons green pepper, chopped
2 tablespoons butter
2 tablespoons flour
½ teaspoon mustard
¼ teaspoon salt
½ teaspoon Worcestershire sauce
¾ cup milk
2 or 3 cups crab meat, cooked
Dash cayenne pepper
1 cup stewed, strained tomatoes
1 cup Cheddar cheese, grated
1 egg, slightly beaten

Cook green pepper in butter 5 minutes; blend in flour, add seasonings, tomatoes, egg, and cheese; cook a few minutes. Heat the milk before adding to the other ingredients, then add crab meat (either canned or fresh frozen crab may be used).

Serve in patty shells or on rounds of toast. Save 1 tablespoon cheese to sprinkle on top.

Mustard Sauce for Ham

½ cup tomato soup
½ cup prepared mustard
½ cup vinegar
½ cup sugar
½ cup butter
3 egg yolks, slightly beaten

Cook over water in double boiler until mixture thickens and eggs are cooked. Serve warm over baked ham. Will keep in refrigerator.

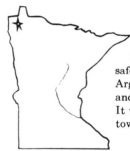

MARSHALL COUNTY for years played "Who has the safe?" There was a battle for the county seat between Argyle and Warren. County records were kept in a safe and a sketchy government operated wherever the safe was. It was never anywhere long before the folks of the other town went raiding. In an election, finally, Warren won.

Krumb Kag (Scandinavian)

1 cup sugar
½ cup butter
2 eggs
1 cup milk
1½ cups flour
1 teaspoon vanilla or a little cardamom can be used if desired

Mix together in order given and bake on a krumb kag iron. When baked, roll on a round stick. Makes about 60.

Soft Gingerbread

Here's a gingerbread which bakes with a crumb soft as feathers, a bread tender, one deliciously flavored of the molasses. I received this recipe from a friend whose mother remembers carrying squares of this cake for lunch to a country school held in the loft of a neighbor's barn.

Eventually this cake was made by the entire neighborhood. The recipe was passed from hand to hand and along with it very often went a gift hen and a setting of eggs. Mrs. Helmer Johnson, Strathcona.

1 cup shortening
1 cup sugar
1 cup molasses
2 teaspoons soda
1 cup sour milk
2½ cups sifted all-purpose flour
1 teaspoon ginger
1 teaspoon cinnamon
1 teaspoon allspice
4 eggs

Cream shortening and sugar. Stir in molasses. Stir soda into sour milk and add alternately to the creamed mixture with the flour which has been sifted with the spices. Beat in the 4 eggs, one at a time. Pour into 2 greased and floured 9" x 12" pans or 2 large skillets. Bake at 325 degrees 45 to 55 minutes.

Spiced Nuts

1 pound shelled nuts
2 cups sugar
1 cup cornstarch
1 teaspoon salt
1 teaspoon nutmeg
2 teaspoons allspice
1 teaspoon ginger
6 teaspoons cinnamon
2 egg whites
4 tablespoons water

Blanch nuts, if necessary. Sift together dry ingredients and spread on a platter. Beat egg whites slightly, add water and beat again. Add nuts and stir until all are coated with egg mixture. Roll nuts in dry ingredients. Place on a cookie sheet, keeping nuts apart. Bake at 250 degrees 1 hour. Cool, store in airtight tins.

Boiled Cabbage and Side Pork

This recipe has been handed down for 4 generations in my family since 1857. It was used by my grandmother as an annual New Year's Eve dish in Denmark. Mrs. Peder Moe, Argyle.

2 pounds fresh side pork
1 large head cabbage
2 teaspoons salt

Boil the side pork in water to cover, add salt. You may either leave the pork in one piece or slice it, as you like. Boil 40 minutes and slice the cabbage and put on top, cover and let boil or steam for 30 minutes more.

Brunswick Chicken

2½ cups boiled rice
2 cups cooked chicken
¼ cup onion, chopped
¼ cup pimiento, chopped
2 tablespoons green pepper, chopped
2 tablespoons butter or chicken fat
2 cups chicken broth
Salt and pepper
⅔ cup mushrooms

Melt butter in skillet, add flour, chicken broth and cook until smooth. Add rest of ingredients and put in a buttered baking dish. Cover with toasted crumbs. Bake 30 minutes at 350 degrees.

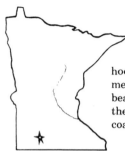

MARTIN COUNTY once knew the pink coats and flying hoofs of fox-hunting. Fairmont was colonized by Englishmen, some titled, who planned to make fortunes growing beans. The grasshopper plague wiped out the beans but the Britishers survived. Clad in their boots and fancy coats, they put on a sensational show at the 1878 state fair.

100 Year Favorite Fruit Cake

2 cups raisins
2 cups dates, chopped
2 cups brown sugar
2 cups water
5 tablespoons shortening
1 teaspoon cinnamon
1 teaspoon cloves
1 teaspoon soda
½ teaspoon salt
1 cup walnut meats, chopped
1 cup thick applesauce
½ pound mixed fruit
2 cups flour

Cook raisins, dates, brown sugar, water, and shortening 20 minutes and cool. Add remaining ingredients. Bake for 2 hours in slow oven (300 degrees).

Casserole Meal

2 medium-sized onions, sliced thin
4 medium-sized potatoes, sliced thin
2 cups corn (fresh, canned, or frozen)
1 pound bulk pork sausage
1 cup tomato sauce
½ teaspoon salt
⅛ teaspoon pepper
Dash paprika

Grease a casserole and place the ingredients in it, in the order given. The sausage is made into balls or patties, and the tomato sauce is poured over all. Cover and bake in a moderate (350 degrees) oven for 30 minutes. Remove the cover and bake until potatoes are tender and the dish nicely browned.

Pumpkin Fruit Roll

2 cups flour
¾ teaspoon salt
4 teaspoons baking powder
2 tablespoons lard or other shortening
¾ cup milk

Sift flour, salt, baking powder together. Cut in lard, add milk. Roll into an oblong and spread with following filling. Roll as for jelly roll. Place upside down in greased tin or on cookie sheet and bake in moderate oven (350 degrees) 45 minutes or until biscuit crust is done.

Filling

1 cup pumpkin
2 tablespoons molasses
½ cup sugar
⅛ teaspoon salt
¼ cup nuts, chopped
1 cup raisins
½ teaspoon cinnamon
½ teaspoon nutmeg
1 teaspoon vanilla
2 tablespoons flour

Combine and cook over slow fire until thick.

Orange Candy Cookies

1½ cups brown sugar (firmly packed)
½ cup fat
2 eggs
2 cups flour
1 teaspoon soda
¼ teaspoon salt
½ pound orange candy, diced
½ cup flour
½ cup flaked coconut or chopped nuts
½ cup rolled oats

Cream brown sugar and fat until light and fluffy. Beat in eggs. Sift flour, soda, and salt together and blend in. Fold in diced orange candy which has been mixed with ½ cup of flour. Add coconut and rolled oats. Mix well and roll in 1″ balls. Place on greased cookie sheet and press with a fork. Bake at 325 degrees for 12 minutes. Makes 6 dozen cookies.

MEEKER COUNTY early became a grain growing area. The farmers fed hogs and beef cattle, but had to sell them to private buyers who would guess the weight of the animals, to the disadvantage of the farmers. Butter, made in the homes, was bartered for staples. At Litchfield, creameries started in the 1890's pioneered in the co-operative movement.

Boston Brown Bread

2 cups sour milk
¾ cup molasses
1 cup bran
1 cup whole-wheat flour
1 cup corn meal
2 teaspoons soda
2 tablespoons sugar
1½ teaspoons salt
1 teaspoon cinnamon
1 cup raisins

Combine sour milk, molasses, and bran; let stand about 10 minutes or until most of the liquid is absorbed by the bran. Combine dry ingredients and raisins; fold into bran mixture and stir just enough to moisten the dry ingredients. Do not beat.

Fill greased molds ⅔ full; recipe will fill 3 1-quart molds or 2 1½-quart molds. Cover with greased close-fitting covers, heavy waxed paper or parchment paper; steam about 3 hours. Uncover and bake in a slow oven (250 degrees) for 20 to 30 minutes or until tops are dry. Remove from molds and serve hot; to serve later, simply re-steam in molds until hot.

Chess Pie

Pastry for 1 pie shell
½ cup butter, creamed
1 cup sugar
3 whole eggs plus 1 egg white
½ cup nuts, chopped
½ cup milk
1 cup dates, chopped
1 cup raisins, chopped
½ teaspoon vanilla

Blend in order given and bake in a rich pie crust at 425 degrees for 35 to 40 minutes. Cool. Top with whipped cream when ready to serve.

Red Currant Cobbler

1 cup white sugar
¾ cup brown sugar
¼ cup butter
1 quart red currants, washed
1 cup white flour
2 teaspoons baking powder
1 egg
⅔ cup milk
3 tablespoons shortening

Put white and brown sugar, butter, and red currants into greased baking dish. Top with a mixture made of the flour, baking powder, egg, and milk. Bake at 425 degrees for 25 to 30 minutes. Serve warm, with cream.

Partridge Pie

2 or 3 partridge breasts
1 medium-sized onion, sliced
1 cup water
3 whole allspice
6 carrots, cooked and chopped
  Salt, pepper
  Paprika
  Biscuit dough

Sprinkle breasts with salt and pepper, roll in flour and paprika and brown well in hot shortening. Add sliced onion and fry a few minutes longer. Add water and allspice, cover and simmer until well done, about 1½ to 2 hours. Add more water if it cooks away. Remove meat from pan. Add water enough to make at least 1 quart. (Milk or chicken stock may be used to make a richer gravy.) Thicken with a paste of flour and water. Add more salt and pepper if needed. Put meat and hot, cooked carrots in a casserole and pour gravy over them. Make biscuits and place close together over meat in casserole. Sprinkle with paprika and bake at 425 degrees for 15 to 20 minutes. Serves 4 to 6.

MILLE LACS COUNTY lies south of the big lake of the same name. Here was once a great Sioux village, named Izatys, which drew early French explorers, among them Sieur du Lhut who claimed the area for Louis XIV in 1679. The next year the Sioux captured Father Louis Hennepin and brought him to the village, firing the grass behind to make him hurry.

Grandmother Schimming's Shortcake

As far as I have been able to determine, this recipe of my grand-mother's was her very own original idea; something which she just "cooked up for supper." I treasure it. Mrs. L. Heckler, Princeton.

> **2 tablespoons sugar**
> **1½ teaspoons baking powder**
> **¼ teaspoon soda**
> **1½ cups sifted flour**
> **½ teaspoon salt**
> **⅓ cup butter**
> **½ to ⅔ cup milk**
> **3 cups fresh or frozen raspberries, thawed**
> **1 cup sugar**
> **1 cup sour or heavy sweet cream**

Sift first 5 dry ingredients, blend in butter and add milk, just enough to make soft dough. Pat into well-buttered glass loaf pan, about 8″ x 12″. Place berries evenly on dough, sprinkle with the sugar and pour cream over all. Bake at 375 degrees 40 to 45 minutes. Serve warm but not hot. Plan to remove from oven about 30 minutes before serving time.

Almond Swedish Rusks

> **1 cup sugar**
> **½ cup butter**
> **2 eggs**
> **1 teaspoon soda**
> **1 cup almonds, ground**
> **½ cup sour cream or buttermilk**
> **3 cups flour (if batter is too sticky, add more)**

Put everything into mixing bowl and mix well. Make 2 long rolls and place on cookie sheet. Bake at 300 degrees about 45 minutes. When light brown take out and cut into ½″ slices. Toast first on one side and then on the other in an oven 250 or 300 degrees until rusks are light brown and crisp, about 30 to 45 minutes in all.

Schoolteacher Pie

1 baked pastry shell
1 dozen large fresh strawberries
¼ pound butter
1 cup flour
¼ teaspoon salt
2 tablespoons milk
1 tablespoon sugar
1 pint whipping cream
¼ teaspoon salt
½ cup sugar
6 egg yolks
1 teaspoon vanilla
1 cup brown sugar

Hull and halve a dozen large fresh strawberries, sugar lightly and let stand. Mix butter, flour, salt, milk, and sugar. This will be crumbly. Press this mixture into bottom and side of shallow pan. Bake in moderate oven (350 degrees) until brown for 30 minutes. Let cool.

Drain the berries well and place them in baked crust. Scald whipping cream in double boiler, add to it salt and sugar. In a bowl beat egg yolks until creamy; pour whipping cream over eggs. Cook in double boiler until mixture coats the spoon. Remove from heat and add vanilla. When it begins to cool, pour this mixture over berries in pie shell. Chill thoroughly. Shortly before serving, sprinkle brown sugar over the top and place under the broiler for 5 minutes or just enough for sugar to melt and form a crust. Chill again. Decorate with 2 or 3 whole berries placed in a small nest of whipped cream in center of the pie.

Baked Steak with Wild Rice

2 pounds steak
2 cups cooked wild rice
½ cup onions, chopped
2 tablespoons fat
¼ cup parsley, chopped
Tomato juice or stock
2 tablespoons flour

Pound steak and season and dredge with flour. Brown onion in fat. Add flour and ¼ cup of stock or tomato juice. Add cooked rice and parsley. Spread on steak, roll and fasten with skewers. Sear well. Add a small amount of tomato juice and bake slowly (275 degrees) for 2 hours.

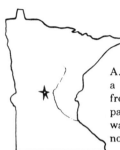

MORRISON COUNTY was the boyhood home of Charles A. Lindbergh, whose family home at Little Falls is now a state park. His father, a lawyer, was a congressman from 1907 to 1917, but his persistent and courageous pacifism made him unpopular after the nation went to war. The county also was the site of old Fort Ripley, now gone.

Apple Raisin Coffee Cake

¾ cup sugar
¼ cup soft shortening
1 egg
1½ cups flour
2 teaspoons baking powder
½ teaspoon salt
½ cup raisins
½ teaspoon vanilla
½ cup milk
Several ripe baking apples
Cinnamon-sugar for topping

Mix shortening, egg, and sugar together well; stir in milk, stir in sifted dry ingredients. Add raisins and vanilla.

Spread batter in greased and floured square or oblong pan. Arrange apple slices (apples may have peelings on if nice and red) in design or rows on top of batter, pressing slightly. Sprinkle top of cake and apples with 1 teaspoon cinnamon which has been mixed with 2 teaspoons sugar. Bake about 25 minutes in 375 degree oven.

Delicious served fresh from oven. For dessert, lemon sauce or whipped cream are desirable. A sprinkling of walnut meats can be added also.

Bakeless Cake

1 cup sugar
1 cup butter
3 egg yolks, beaten
1 No. 2 can crushed pineapple
1 cup nuts, chopped
1 box vanilla wafers
Whipped cream

Mix all of the above together, except wafers. Into an oblong pan place 1 layer of wafers, then a layer of pineapple mixture (use only about ½ of the juice from the canned pineapple). Make 3 layers, with the top layer wafers. Top, if desired, with whipped cream.

Chicken Soufflé

4 tablespoons shortening
4 tablespoons flour
2 cups milk
1½ teaspoons salt
Dash pepper
3 egg yolks, beaten
2 cups cooked chicken, minced
½ teaspoon parsley, finely minced
½ teaspoon onion, finely minced

Make white sauce of first 5 ingredients and pour over beaten egg yolks, stirring constantly. Cool. Add minced chicken, parsley, and onion. Fold in beaten egg whites. Put into well-greased casserole, covering with fine buttered bread crumbs. Set in pan of hot water, and bake at 375 degrees for 45 to 50 minutes.

Potato Dumplings (Norwegian Klub)

4 cups potatoes, ground fine or grated
3 cups flour
2 teaspoons salt
Salt pork or bacon

Mix together and shape into balls the size of an apple. (Shape with your hands dipped first in cold water or flour.) Press a piece of salt pork or bacon into center of each. Drop into salted boiling water and cook for 1 hour, stirring frequently so they don't stick to the bottom of the kettle.

Serve with butter, and they're also very good sliced and fried in butter or shortening for the next meal. These dumplings are an old Norwegian favorite. (Allow two large potatoes per person.)

Rhubarb Pie

1 unbaked 9" pastry
2 cups Minnesota strawberry rhubarb, cut-up
2 egg yolks
1 whole egg, beaten well
1 cup sugar
2 tablespoons flour
3 or 4 tablespoons cream
¼ cup sweet milk
Dash salt

Fill pie crust about ¾ full of rhubarb. Make a custard of remaining ingredients and pour over rhubarb. Bake in medium oven (350 degrees) 50 to 55 minutes. Put a meringue on the last 10 minutes of baking by beating the 2 left-over egg whites with 4 tablespoons sugar.

MOWER COUNTY was one of many that waged a heated fight over the county seat location. It was first at Frankford, but Austin wanted it. Austin won an 1856 election but Frankford wouldn't give up the records. Austin commissioners led a raid and were arrested between towns—but only after they'd hidden the records in a snowbank.

Cabbage Roll (Swedish Kaldolmar)

    1 pound round steak
    ½ pound fresh pork
    8 large cabbage leaves
    1 cup bread crumbs
    ½ cup milk
      Salt and pepper

Parboil the cabbage leaves in plenty of water until limp but not soft. In the meantime grind steak and pork and mix with the bread crumbs, salt and pepper, and milk. Form into oblong rolls about 3″ and lay one in the center of each leaf. Wind carefully with thread and fry slowly until browned on all sides, using butter and drippings. Cover with stock or hot water and cook slowly for about 45 minutes. Remove thread carefully, lay on platter, and pour remaining liquid over.

Blueberry Coffee Cake

    ¾ cup sugar
    ¼ cup shortening
    1 egg
    ½ cup milk
    2 cups sifted flour
    2 teaspoons baking powder
    ½ teaspoon salt
    2 cups blueberries, fresh, or canned,
      and drained
    ½ cup sugar
    ⅓ cup sifted flour
    ½ teaspoon cinnamon
    ¼ cup soft butter

Mix sugar and shortening. Add egg. Sift flour, baking powder and salt. Add with milk. Blend in blueberries. Spread in 9″ square pan and sprinkle with topping made of remaining ingredients. Bake at 375 degrees for 25 to 30 minutes.

Baked Beans with Maple Syrup

In my grandmother's time measurements were not very accurate. She did not use a spoon or a cup to measure her molasses but measured it by the "plop" or "blurp" as it came from the jug. Old recipes sometimes specified how many "plops" to add. Mrs. Ernest Anderson, Adams.

1 quart navy beans
1 pound pork (either salt or fresh; ham hock is fine)
1 onion
½ cup maple syrup
½ teaspoon dry mustard
2 teaspoons salt
2 tablespoons molasses
Boiling water (keep on hand)

Wash beans and put into a large pot for baking. I prepare my beans in the thrift cooker or in my deep fat dryer. Long slow baking is the secret with baked beans.

Nestle onion in the bottom of the pot and pour washed beans over same. Put pork down into beans so that only a small portion shows. Mix syrup, mustard, salt, and molasses with a little water; pour over beans. Pour on boiling water to cover. Bring to boiling point in oven and then reduce to 200 to 250 degrees and keep at that temperature for 6 to 8 hours. Be sure to add a little hot water as needs demand to keep the beans covered all the time.

About ½ hour before serving time add ½ to 1 cup of sweet pickle juice, for a special touch.

Date Nut Loaf

1 teaspoon soda
1 cup dates, cut up
1 cup boiling water
¾ cup brown sugar
¼ teaspoon salt
1 tablespoon butter
1 egg
½ cup walnuts, chopped
1½ cups flour

Sprinkle soda over cut dates. Pour boiling water over both. Combine sugar, salt, butter, and eggs. Add nuts and date mixture and sifted flour. Turn into greased pan. Bake at 300 degrees for 1 hour.

MURRAY COUNTY'S early settlers built log cabins along the eastern shore of Lake Shetek in the 1850's and started to break land. By 1862, there were 50 or more in the settlement when the angry Sioux came, killed many, drove the others out, burned the cabins and ran off all of the livestock.

Carrot Cookies

        ¾ cup sugar
        ¾ cup shortening
        1 egg
        1 cup cooked mashed carrots
        ½ teaspoon salt
        1 teaspoon vanilla
        2 cups flour
        2 level teaspoons baking powder
        Nutmeats

Drop by teaspoonfuls onto cookie sheet. Bake at 375 degrees for 10 minutes. Cool and frost.

        Frosting

        1 cup powdered sugar
        2 teaspoons orange rind, grated
        2 tablespoons orange juice
        1 tablespoon butter

Pineapple Pie

        30 Ritz crackers, crushed
        ¼ cup melted butter
        4 egg yolks, well beaten
        ½ cup sugar
        1 small can pineapple
        ½ box lemon Jello
        4 egg whites, beaten
        ½ cup sugar
        Whipped cream

Make a crust of Ritz crackers and butter. Pat gently into pie plate. Let the crust stand overnight at room temperature.

Make a filling of yolks, sugar, and pineapple. Cook in double boiler until thick. Remove from heat and add Jello. Beat egg whites, add sugar and fold into cooled pineapple mixture. Chill and serve with whipped cream.

Cold Water Fudge Cake

¾ cup butter
2¼ cups sugar
1½ teaspoons vanilla
3 eggs
3 squares unsweetened chocolate
3 cups sifted cake flour
1½ teaspoons baking soda
¾ teaspoon salt
1½ cups ice water

Cream butter, sugar, and vanilla. Add eggs which have been beaten until light and fluffy. Melt chocolate and add to creamed mixture. Sift flour, baking soda and salt together and add to creamed mixture alternately with ice water.

Bake in 3 layers or a large loaf (can use oven broiler pan). Cool and fill with your favorite filling; cover with chocolate frosting.

Dutch Pastry Letter

When I was a young girl and lived in Holland, it was the New Year's Eve custom for a Dutch lad to bring one of these pastries to his sweetheart when he went courting. The pastry would be in the shape of her initial.

Then the girl's mother entered the picture. According to tradition, she made a quantity of cocoa or hot chocolate which they all drank when they ate the Dutch Pastry Letter. Mrs. Petter De Greeff, Chandler.

1½ cups flour
1 cup butter
Enough water to hold together
2½ cups almonds, blanched
1 cup sugar
1 egg white
1 teaspoon lemon juice
1 teaspoon almond extract

Mix crust of flour, butter and water as for pie crust. Put aside, and blanch almonds, then put them through a food chopper (quite fine). Add the rest of the ingredients. Then roll out ½ of the dough about ½" thick and 6" wide. Put ½ of filling in middle of crust and roll both sides around filling. Shape in any letter desired. Close ends and brush top with 1 egg yolk mixed with 1 tablespoon of water. Bake in hot oven (400 degrees) 15 to 20 minutes, then reduce heat to moderate oven (350 degrees) for about 40 minutes. Makes 2 "letters."

NICOLLET COUNTY was named for a French exile who surveyed much of southern Minnesota, making maps and selecting many names now in use. St. Peter, the county seat, wanted to be capital of the new state of Minnesota. A bill to make it so passed the 1857 legislature, but Representative Joe Rolette disappeared with it before it could be engrossed.

Tuna Casserole

6 tablespoons butter or shortening
6 tablespoons flour
3 cups milk
¾ teaspoons salt
Pepper
1 cup American cheese, grated
1 can tuna
¼ cup onion, finely chopped
3 hard-cooked eggs
3 cups cooked potatoes, cubed
1 tablespoon butter
2 tablespoons fine bread crumbs
1 can flaked crabmeat (optional)

Make a white sauce of flour, shortening, and milk. Add seasonings and cheese. Put a layer of tuna in bottom of greased casserole. Sprinkle with onions, then add a layer of half of the potatoes. Pour half of the cheese sauce over this. Add a layer of sliced eggs and crabmeat, then put on the rest of the potatoes. Pour remaining white sauce over all, and sprinkle with bread crumbs and butter. Bake in an uncovered casserole for 45 minutes at 350 degrees. Serves 10.

Spring Salad

1 package lemon Jello
2 tablespoons lemon juice
1 teaspoon salt
¼ cup spring onions, sliced
½ cup radishes, diced
½ cup cucumber, diced
½ cup celery, diced

Set lemon Jello in the usual way, adding lemon juice and salt to the liquid. Refrigerate until slightly thickened. Add remaining ingredients, pour into mold and refrigerate until firm.

Scrambled Vegetables on Toast

¼ cup butter
3 small onions, sliced
¼ green pepper, chopped
2 eggs
1½ cups corn
1½ cups tomatoes
1 cup cooked carrots, chopped
1 teaspoon salt
¼ teaspoon paprika
¼ cup flour

Melt butter, add onions, and pepper. Cook slowly until tender. Blend in flour, then add corn, tomatoes, and carrots. Season with salt. Simmer for 15 minutes, stirring frequently. Beat eggs, add and cook for 2 minutes. Serve on hot, crisp, buttered toast.

Grandmother's Kratser

Before Minnesota became a State, my grandmother kept what was known as a Halfway House between New Ulm and St. Peter. Tired and weary travelers stopped at the Halfway House at all hours of the day, and often at night. Some were on their way to new homes, and others arrived with much-needed provisions, for New Ulm was just a frontier out-post at that time.

Grandmother's food supply often ran low, but she kept chickens so she usually had eggs. When bread, meat, and potatoes were gone, she would stir up her specialty. Making a batter of eggs, flour, and water, she would heat some pork-crackles in an iron skillet, pour the batter over the crackles, and as it browned she would scrape or scratch, and turn the batter, making uneven little golden omelets.

Because she scraped or scratched the pan, she called her specialty, "Kratser," the German word for scratching. Louise Bower, St. Paul.

3 eggs
½ cup milk
½ cup flour
Season to taste
Bacon (or pork crackles)

Make a batter of the above and stir briskly. Cut bacon into 2″ pieces and brown in skillet. Pour off fat. Pour batter over bacon and let bubble until nicely browned. Then cut in pieces and turn so they will brown on all sides. They will be uneven little delicious omelets. Serve plain or with maple syrup.

NOBLES COUNTY is part of a region known nationally for its elegant turkeys. Those toothsome fowls annually reign over Turkey Day in Worthington, the county seat. Worthington, on Lake Okabena (which means "the nesting place of herons"), was started as a prohibition colony. Original deeds forbade the sale of liquor.

Wine Soup

> 3 cups hot water
> ⅔ cup sugar
> ⅔ cup sago or ½ cup minute tapioca
> ¼ teaspoon salt
> ¼ cup cider vinegar
> ½ cup sweet grape wine
> 1 cup raisins (washed)

Combine water, sugar, sago or tapioca, and salt and cook in heavy sauce pan until sago or tapioca is clear. Then add remaining ingredients, stir and let come to a boil. Serve piping hot in soup bowls.

Saffron Fruit Bread (English)

> 2 tablespoons of Spanish saffron
> 1½ cups boiling water
> 2 packages yeast
> ½ cup warm water
> 10 to 12 cups flour
> 2 scant cups sugar
> 1½ tablespoons salt
> 1⅛ cups shortening, warmed
> 2 cups raisins
> 1½ cups currants
> 1 cup dried fruits, cut up
> 2 eggs, beaten

Warm the flour and add sugar, salt, shortening, and soaked currants and raisins and cut fruits. Soak yeast in a little warm water. Steep saffron in boiling water and let cool until lukewarm. Strain and use the tea as liquid for bread, adding the beaten eggs. Mix the yeast, saffron tea, and eggs into the flour mixture as for bread. It will be a golden yellow. Knead and let rise in warm place covered with towel. When doubled in bulk, make into biscuits or loaves and let rise (covered) again. Bake at 400 degrees until crust browns and then reduce heat and bake like bread until done.

Molasses Cookies

The keynote of the hospitality of the early German pioneers was simplicity. When friends called, black oolong tea was served. The tea cups were filled, placed on their saucers and passed to guests as they sat in their chairs. Then the cream and sugar were passed. The spoons were hooked on the sugar bowl, in case you used sugar. The cups were refilled at intervals until the cup was turned upside down, indicating that the guest had had enough. Many a guest found himself drinking more tea than he wanted because his cup remained right side up.

Since molasses was a common household commodity, molasses cookies were popular for teatime. Mrs. William Fagerness, Rushmore.

1 cup lard
2 cups sugar
3 unbeaten eggs
1 teaspoon soda
½ cup hot water
½ cup molasses
1 teaspoon nutmeg
¼ teaspoon cloves
1 teaspoon cinnamon
1 teaspoon salt
1 cup raisins
Flour to roll

Cream lard and sugar. Add eggs, dissolve soda in hot water and add to creamed mixture together with remaining ingredients, including adequate flour to make of rolling consistency. Roll out, cut and bake at 375 degrees, 10 to 15 minutes.

Corn Pudding

6 large ears yellow corn
1 teaspoon salt
1 cup near-hot water
3 eggs
⅔ cup clover honey
1 cup milk

Roll the corn over old-style grater until kernels are broken open. With the back of silver knife, force out the corn, leaving the skins on the cob. Add salt and water, bring to a boil, stirring constantly until thickened. Add custard made of remaining ingredients and bake in slow oven (250 degrees) 1 hour.

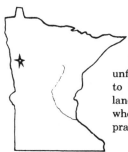

NORMAN COUNTY has no lakes, no swamps, no land unfit for cultivation. That brought settlers who wanted to build farm homes for their families on government land and cheap railroad land. They started an ocean of wheat. Ada, the county seat, is in the midst of a vast prairie where mirages can sometimes be seen on hot days.

Fruit Fritters

> 3 egg yolks
> ½ cup sugar
> 1 cup sweet milk
> ½ teaspoon salt
> 2 teaspoons baking powder
> 1 teaspoon vanilla extract
> ½ teaspoon almond extract
> 2½ cups flour
> 1½ cups dates, cut up fine
> ½ cup nuts
> ½ cup maraschino cherries, cut up

Cream yolks and sugar, add milk, vanilla, and almond. To flour add salt, baking powder and then add to milk mixture, but do not mix yet. Flour fruit a little and add to milk mixture. Then stir all until just mixed. With a teaspoon drop as you would soup dumplings into hot lard (325 degrees). These should be the size of an egg when fried. Drain on paper napkins. Can be served plain or with powdered sugar, as a doughnut.

Barbecued Left-over Chicken or Pheasant

Skin the cooked meat. Cut chicken or pheasant into serving pieces and place in a casserole dish or any covered pan.

> 1 can tomato soup
> 4 tablespoons vinegar
> 2 tablespoons Worcestershire sauce
> 4 tablespoons sugar
> 1 teaspoon salt
> 1 small onion, chopped fine
> Chili powder and black pepper to taste

Pour part of the sauce over the meat and bake either in a medium oven (350 degrees) or on electric fry pan for about 1 hour. Just before serving, add more sauce.

Ginger Snaps

1½ cups sugar
¾ cup butter
2 eggs, beaten well
¾ cup molasses
3½ cups flour
1 teaspoon ginger
1 teaspoon cinnamon
4 teaspoons baking soda
¼ teaspoon salt

Cream sugar and butter; add eggs and beat well. Add molasses; sift flour and spices together and add to creamed mixture.

Roll dough in small balls. Flatten in palm of hands. Bake at 375 degrees, for 8 to 10 minutes.

Cinnamon Twist

1 cake compressed yeast
½ cup milk
2 cups sifted flour
½ cup shortening
1 beaten egg
4 teaspoons sugar
½ teaspoon salt

Dissolve yeast in milk, which has been scalded and then cooled to lukewarm. Sift flour, salt, and sugar. Add shortening to flour and then add yeast and milk mixture. Add eggs. Put dough in wet cloth, tie loosely and place in ice cold water for 1 hour. Scrape dough out on a mixture of ½ cup sugar and 1 tablespoon of cinnamon. Roll until mixture is used up and then form into twists. Place in pan and let rise about ½ hour. Bake 20 minutes at 375 degrees.

Fish Soup

1 pound fish
1 medium onion
1 cup cream
Salt and pepper, to taste
Dash of nutmeg

Cover fish with boiling water in saucepan and simmer 15 minutes. Carefully take fish out and remove the skin and center bone. Break fish into bits and put back into fish stock. Add cream and seasoning and bring to a boil. Serve hot.

OLMSTED COUNTY'S chief fame dates to 1883 when Catholic nuns offered to build a hospital for a local British-born doctor. That was the start of St. Mary's hospital and the Mayo clinic of Rochester. The first Dr. Mayo started his sons' medical education when they were boys, using an old Sioux skeleton for anatomy lessons.

Onion Soup

½ onion per person, sliced very thin
2 tablespoons olive oil
⅛ teaspoon cloves
⅛ teaspoon cinnamon
   Sprinkle of salt, pepper, and flour
   Butter, size of hazel nut
1 cup bouillon per person
1 tablespoon Parmesan cheese, grated
1 tablespoon Swiss cheese, grated
2 tablespoons A-1 sauce
1 tablespoon Worcestershire sauce
¾ cup red wine (Burgundy)
2 tablespoons catsup
1 jigger sherry
   Croutons

Brown onions slowly in oil, using as little oil as possible. Add cloves, cinnamon, salt, pepper, flour, and butter. Continue stirring. Slowly add bouillon. After 10 minutes of simmering, add remaining ingredients, except for catsup, sherry, and croutons. Let simmer ¾ hour. Add catsup and sherry at the very last. Put soup in dishes, add croutons and a little more cheese. Put in oven and broil briefly; serve.

Marshmallow Whip

½ pound marshmallows, cut in fourths
1 cup whipping cream, beaten stiff
2 egg whites, stiffly beaten
1 cup walnuts, coarsely chopped
1 heaping tablespoon powdered sugar
   Pinch salt

Mix these ingredients and let stand at least 3 hours in refrigerator before serving. Top each serving with a dab of whipped cream and a cherry.

Apple Kuchen

1 tablespoon salt
1 cup sugar
2 cups hot water
1 cup condensed milk
2 cakes compressed yeast
2 eggs, beaten
4 rounded tablespoons lard, melted
10 cups flour
½ cup sugar
1 egg
Cinnamon

Pour hot water on salt and sugar. Add milk and cool to luke-warm. Add yeast. Sift flour into large bowl, add yeast mixture, beaten eggs, and melted lard. Mix and turn out on floured board and knead until smooth. Put in greased bowl, grease on top and cover with waxed paper and cloth and let rise in a warm place until very light or three times its size.

Cut off a piece of dough slightly larger than pie crust (as this will be a little thicker than pie crust). Either lay it on a greased pie pan and press into shape with fingers or roll out on board the size of the pie pan. Let rise until light or about 30 minutes. Peel and quarter apples and slice about ¼" thick and lay in rows in circles starting on the outside edge.

Beat sugar and egg and spoon over apples; sprinkle with cinnamon. Bake in a slow oven (350 degrees) for 45 minutes or until apples are done.

Marinade for Steak

For small steak for two, put ½ teaspoon salt into a bowl and mash 1 clove garlic into it. Add 1 tablespoon salad oil, 1 tablespoon Worcestershire sauce and 2 tablespoons red wine vinegar. Add a good dash of Tabasco and mix well.

Pour over steak, turn it and let stand until ready to drain and broil. No more seasoning is needed.

Brandied Peaches in Creme de Cacao

1 pint sour cream
1 quart jar brandied peaches
3 tablespoons creme de cacao

Chill peaches. Before serving, drain fruit and combine juice with creme de cacao and sour cream. Pour sauce over peaches.

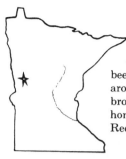

OTTER TAIL COUNTY with more than 1,000 lakes has been a fisherman's paradise since the days when Indians around beautiful Otter Tail lake used dried cornsilk in broth to take the place of salt. Later, white settlers built homes around the lake, too, and heard the loud creaking of Red River oxcarts on the trail that skirted the lake.

Minnesota Rocks

        2 eggs
        1 cup sugar
        ¾ cup butter
        2 cups raisins
        2 tablespoons baking powder
        1 cup walnuts
        3 cups flour or enough to make rocks stiff

Drop by teaspoonful onto buttered pan. Bake at 350 degrees 10-12 minutes.

Old-fashioned Buttermilk Donuts

        1 cup sugar
        4 tablespoons melted shortening
        2 eggs
        2 cups buttermilk
        ¼ teaspoon salt
        ¼ teaspoon cinnamon or nutmeg
        1 teaspoon baking soda
        Enough flour to roll out easily

Mix in order given; roll out and cut. Fry in hot lard until golden.

Date Balls

        1 cup dates
        ½ cup sugar
        1 egg, well beaten
        2 cups Rice Krispies
        ½ cup nuts, chopped
        ¼ teaspoon vanilla
        Coconut

Cook dates, sugar, and egg until thick; add remaining ingredients. Form into balls and roll in coconut. Chill.

Roquefort Cheese Dressing

¼ pound Roquefort cheese, grated
2 tablespoons vinegar
1 teaspoon salt
1 teaspoon Worcestershire sauce
½ pint mayonnaise
1 tablespoon chives, finely chopped, or
tops of green onions

Mix Roquefort cheese, vinegar, salt, and Worcestershire sauce into a smooth paste. Add remaining ingredients and mix well.

Mayonnaise may be increased to cut down on sharp cheese taste. This will keep in refrigerator for at least 1 week.

Gypsy Meat Balls

6 slices bread
½ cup milk
½ pound ground beef
⅛ teaspoon pepper
1 teaspoon salt
1 tablespoon onion, minced
¾ cup sour cream

Pour milk over bread and let stand 15 minutes. Press excess milk out of bread. Combine meat, bread, onion, salt, pepper. Shape into round flat cakes. Fry in skillet in which a little fat has been melted. When browned on both sides, pour cream over meat balls. Simmer about 5 minutes. Arrange on hot platter around cooked vegetables. Serve sauce from pan over meat. Makes about eight 2″ meat balls.

Seafood Supreme

2 cans condensed cream of mushroom
soup, undiluted
1 can thawed frozen shrimp soup
½ cup mushrooms
4 cups any combination of seafood
(shrimp, lobster, crab)
¼ cup sherry
Salt and pepper to taste
Paprika

Combine soups, mushrooms, sherry, salt, pepper, paprika, and lastly add seafood. Place in casserole and put in moderate oven (350 degrees) until heated through. This can be served on fluffy rice.

PENNINGTON COUNTY'S seat, Thief River Falls, was the site of a camp of Sioux who tried to hide from the Chippewa by building a high bank of earth around their lodges. It didn't work. From the mound, the Chippewa gave the river the name, Secret Earth river. Through the years, changes in pronunciation resulted in its being called Stealing Earth, then finally Thief River Falls.

Fudgens (Drop doughnut)

    1 quart milk
    10 tablespoons cornstarch
    2 cups warm water
    1 cake yeast
    2 teaspoons salt
    1 cup sugar
    ½ cup melted butter
    2 eggs, beaten
    1 cup raisins
    8-10 cups flour

Scald milk and thicken with cornstarch. Let cool. In bowl, dissolve yeast in water, add 2 cups flour, salt, sugar, butter, well-beaten eggs, and raisins. Add the two mixtures, then enough flour for a stiff batter. Let rise 2 to 3 hours and drop by spoonfuls into hot grease and fry. May be rolled in sugar. Makes at least 6 dozen.

Coconut Chews

    1 cup flour
    2 tablespoons sugar
    ½ cup butter

Mix above ingredients and pat into bottom of 8" x 13" pan. Bake 10 to 12 minutes in 350 degree oven.

    Filling

    2 beaten eggs
    1½ cups brown sugar
    1 teaspoon vanilla
    2 tablespoons flour
    ¼ teaspoon salt
    ½ cup nuts, chopped
    ½ cup coconut

Pour above filling over the baked crust and return pan to oven and bake 20 minutes. Cool and cut into bars.

Rum Pudding

½ **package dates, cut up fine**
1 **to 2 ounces of rum**
1 **cup walnuts, chopped**
1 **pound marshmallows, cut up**
6 **tablespoons powdered sugar**
2 **cups heavy cream, whipped**
1 **teaspoon vanilla**

Soak dates 1 hour in rum. Whip cream, add sugar, and vanilla. Fold into it the other ingredients. Place in freezer 3 to 4 hours. Will keep indefinitely.

Frozen Ginger Cookies

½ **cup butter**
½ **cup lard**
1 **cup molasses**
1 **cup white sugar**
1 **cup brown sugar**
2 **eggs, beaten**
2 **tablespoons ginger**
1 **teaspoon salt**
½ **teaspoon cinnamon**
1 **teaspoon soda**
4 **cups flour**

Cook first 5 ingredients to a liquid without boiling. Cool and add eggs, flour, and spices. Freeze, slice and bake at 350 to 375 degrees for 8 to 10 minutes.

Whipped Cream Krumkake

1 **cup sugar**
½ **cup butter (do not substitute)**
3 **eggs**
½ **cup whipping cream**
1½ **cups flour plus 1 tablespoon**
½ **teaspoon almond extract**

Beat eggs until very light, add sugar and beat until light and fluffy. Add melted butter and whipped cream and extract. Add flour. Place 1 teaspoon of dough on krumkake iron and bake. When done, roll on stick or form into patty shells.

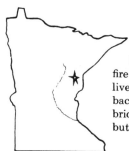

PINE COUNTY was the scene of the sweeping forest fire that wiped out the Hinckley area in 1894, taking 413 lives. One hero was the Northern Pacific engineer who backed his train through a wall of flames across a burning bridge and all the way to Duluth. He saved 350 lives, but his hands were burned fast to the throttle.

Open-faced Kolaches (Bohemian prune buns)

¼ cup lukewarm water
1 cup yeast
1 cup warm milk
½ cup butter
½ cup sugar
1 teaspoon salt
3 eggs
5 cups sifted flour
Prunes, pitted, chopped, sweetened

Mix all ingredients into a soft dough. When light, roll out to ¼″ thickness. Cut into 3″ rounds. Let rise in pan, allowing room to spread. Press down center to form ridge around edge. Brush edges with butter. Place 1 tablespoon pitted, chopped, and sweetened prunes in center. Sprinkle with streusel. Let rise until double in bulk. Bake at 400 degrees, 15 to 20 minutes.

Streusel Topping

2 tablespoons butter
3 tablespoons flour
4 tablespoons sugar

Swedish Omelet

4 eggs, separated
1 cup milk
1 tablespoon flour
½ teaspoon salt
⅛ teaspoon pepper
1 tablespoon fat (not butter)

Beat whites stiff. To the egg yolks add pepper, salt, flour and beat well. Fold in whites of eggs. Pour the mixture into a large frying pan that has been heated with fat. Cook over low heat until well browned on the bottom. Place in oven a few minutes to dry and brown the top. Gently cut through the top and fold over.

This is excellent as is, or with cheese sauce or one of the cream soups heated and poured over it after it is on the platter.

Anise Cookies

                4 cups molasses
                2 cups shortening (not butter)
                ½ cup sugar
                1 teaspoon cinnamon
                1 teaspoon anise oil
                ½ teaspoon salt
                4 teaspoons soda
                ¼ cup hot water
                Flour sufficient to make dough roll

Warm shortening and molasses together; add sugar. Dissolve soda in hot water and add with remaining ingredients.

Cut in fancy shapes. Bake at 350 degrees. Frost before serving with a powdered sugar icing and decorate with colored sprinkles.

Lemon Halo Cookies

                2 cups sifted flour
                1 teaspoon salt
                1 teaspoon soda
                ½ cup shortening
                1 cup brown sugar
                1 teaspoon vanilla
                1 egg

Mix and chill. Shape dough into ball and flatten ⅛" thick on cookie sheet. Place a teaspoonful of meringue on cookie. Hollow out meringue with a teaspoon dipped in cold water. Bake in 300 degree oven, 10 to 12 minutes. Fill with lemon filling.

                Meringue

                3 egg whites
                ¾ cup sugar
                2 tablespoons lemon juice

Beat egg whites until foamy, add sugar and beat stiff. Add lemon juice,

                Filling

                3 egg yolks
                1 cup sugar
                ¼ cup lemon juice
                1 teaspoon lemon rind

Heat to boiling point and add 3 tablespoons butter.

PIPESTONE COUNTY'S quarries are famous in Indian lore as the source of the odd reddish stone used to make peace pipes. The treasured pipes were bartered to various tribes and have been found in burial grounds in several states. Indians believed that the Great Spirit created man at the quarries, and that the red stone was the hardened flesh of their ancestors.

Bacon Muffins

2 cups sifted flour
3 teaspoons baking powder
½ teaspoon salt
3 tablespoons sugar
1 egg, well beaten
1 cup milk
4 tablespoons shortening, melted
7 strips bacon, cooked and crumbled

Sift dry ingredients together into bowl. Combine liquid ingredients and add to flour mixture. Stir only enough to partially dampen flour. Add bacon and stir only enough to blend. Fill greased muffin pan ⅔ full. Bake at 375 degrees for 30 minutes.

Mystery Mocha Cake

¾ cup sugar
1 cup sifted all-purpose flour
2 teaspoons baking powder
½ teaspoon salt
1 square unsweetened chocolate
2 tablespoons butter
½ cup milk
1 teaspoon vanilla
½ cup brown sugar, firmly packed
½ cup granulated sugar
¼ cup cocoa
1 cup cold coffee

Sift first 4 ingredients together. Melt chocolate and butter; add to first mixture. Blend well. Combine milk and vanilla; add to mixture and mix well. Pour batter into greased 8″ x 8″ x 2″ pan. Combine brown and granulated sugars and cocoa. Sprinkle over batter. Pour coffee over top of batter. Bake in 350 degree oven 40 minutes. Serve warm or cold, and cake may be topped with whipped cream.

Cranberry Crumble

1 cup sugar
1 cup water
2 cups fresh cranberries
1 tablespoon orange rind, grated
⅔ cup prunes, cooked and chopped
¼ cup flour
¼ cup sugar
¼ cup butter
2 cups corn flakes, crushed

Combine sugar and water in saucepan. Bring to a boil; add cranberries and continue cooking for 5 minutes or until cranberries burst. Add orange rind and prunes. Pour into a 1½-quart casserole. Combine flour and sugar; work in butter with fork until crumbly; add corn flakes and toss. Sprinkle over fruit mixture. Bake at 400 degrees for 45 minutes. This may be served with whipped cream.

Chicken Loaf

1 4-pound chicken, cooked and
    cut from bone
1 cup rice, cooked
⅛ cup pimiento, chopped
2 cups fresh bread crumbs
1½ teaspoons salt
3 cups milk or milk and chicken broth
4 eggs

Mix chicken, rice, pimiento, bread crumbs, salt, and liquid. Add the eggs, well beaten. Bake at 325 degrees for about 1 hour. Serve with sauce.

Sauce

¼ cup butter
½ pound can mushrooms
¼ cup flour
1 pint chicken broth
½ cup cream
⅛ teaspoon paprika
½ teaspoon lemon juice
½ tablespoon parsley, chopped
Salt to taste

Melt butter, add mushrooms, and cook 5 minutes. Add rest of ingredients and cook until thick and smooth.

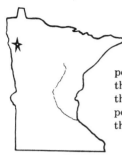

POLK COUNTY a champion producer of wheat, barley, potatoes and sugar beets, was part of the famous trail of the squeaking wooden-wheeled Red River oxcarts. Along the trail is a giant cottonwood used by old settlers as a post office. Letters were left in a box to be picked up by the trail drivers.

Springerle (German-Swiss cookies)

If you do not have a springerle rolling pin with its little imprints of leaves, etc., there are other ways to make the prints. Take old buttermolds, or an old jelly glass, or an old-fashioned dish, and press against the cookies to make an imprint.

2 cups sugar
4 eggs
4 cups flour
10 drops anise oil
2 tablespoons anise seed

Add sugar gradually to well-beaten eggs and continue to beat for 15 minutes with electric beater or 30 minutes with rotary beater. Add anise oil. Gradually add sifted flour and stir until a smooth, stiff dough is formed. Chill dough.

Roll out ¼" thick on lightly-floured board. Then roll with springerle roller to make designs. Press firmly and cut in small squares (design in center of cookie). Place cookies 1" apart on ungreased sheet. Sprinkle with anise seeds; let stand in a cool place overnight to dry. Bake at 375 degrees for 3 minutes, then reduce to 325 degrees for 12 minutes.

When baked, these cookies should be light in color and appear frosted. Keep cookies in a tight can for 2 or 3 weeks before using. To soften cookie, put an apple in container a day or so before they are served. Makes 4 dozen.

Delicious Green Beans

1 No. 2 can green beans
1 small onion, chopped
5 slices bacon
1 can mushroom soup
3 tablespoons cream

Fry bacon until crisp. Cook onion at same time until tender. Drain fat off bacon and add bacon to the mushroom soup that has been diluted with the cream. Add onions and heat. When hot, add the beans which have been thoroughly drained. Simmer for 10 minutes.

Sugar Cake (Moravian)

1 package active dry or 1 cake yeast
¼ cup warm water
½ cup granulated sugar
¼ teaspoon salt
½ cup butter, melted
1 egg, well beaten
½ cup hot mashed potato (may use instant)
2¾ cups sifted flour
¼ cup light brown sugar, packed
2 tablespoons butter, melted
½ teaspoon cinnamon
1½ teaspoons water
⅓ cup sifted confectioner's sugar
1 teaspoon hot water
¼ teaspoon vanilla

In large bowl crumble yeast into warm water. Stir until yeast is dissolved. Stir in granulated sugar, salt, ½ cup melted butter, egg, mashed potato.

Blend thoroughly; add half flour, beat until smooth. Add remaining flour and mix well. Cover bowl with clean cloth, then damp towel and let stand in cool place 12 hours.

Turn dough into greased 9″ x 9″ x 2″ pan and spread with floured fingers. Start heating oven to 400 degrees. Meanwhile, combine brown sugar, melted butter, cinnamon, and water. With thumb, make shallow impressions in dough about 1″ apart; spoon some of brown sugar mixture into each.

Bake cake 20 to 25 minutes or until done; cool, then drizzle with combined confectioner's sugar, hot water, and vanilla.

Candy Apple Pie

6 medium-sized green, tart apples,
    cored and pared
½ teaspoon cinnamon
½ cup brown sugar
1 teaspoon lemon juice
1 cup flour
1 cup brown sugar
¼ teaspoon salt
¼ pound butter (room temperature)
½ cup walnuts, coarsely chopped

Pare apples into 9″ buttered pie tin; sprinkle cinnamon and ½ cup brown sugar and lemon juice over apples.

In separate bowl place flour, brown sugar, salt, and butter and mix until well blended. Add nuts and place on top of apples. Press firmly. Bake at 350 degrees 50 to 60 minutes. Serve with ice cream.

POPE COUNTY is named for General John Pope of Sioux and Civil war fame. He was one of the explorers in this area in 1849 and camped near Lake Minnewaska where Glenwood, the county seat, now stands. Near the lake are Indian mounds and burial grounds containing graves of Chief White Bear and the Princess Minnewaska.

Old-fashioned Pepparkakor (Swedish cookie)

3½ cups sifted flour
1 teaspoon soda
1½ teaspoons ginger
1½ teaspoons cinnamon
1 teaspoon ground cloves
¼ teaspoon ground cardamom
   (may be omitted, if desired)
½ cup butter
¾ cup sugar
1 unbeaten egg
¾ cup molasses
2 teaspoons orange rind, grated
Blanched almond halves, if desired

Sift together flour, soda, ginger, cinnamon, cloves, and cardamom. Cream butter. Gradually add sugar, creaming until light and fluffy. Add egg, molasses, and orange rind; beat well. Gradually stir in dry ingredients, mixing until well blended. Cover. Chill overnight. (Dough may be used in small amounts. Will keep 1 week.) Roll out on well-floured pastry board or cloth to ⅛" thickness. Cut into various shapes with cookie cutters. Place on greased baking sheet. If desired, place a blanched almond half in center of each cookie. Bake in moderate oven (375 degrees) 8 to 10 minutes. Makes 7 to 8 dozen cookies.

Best Brownies in America

½ cup butter
1 cup sugar
2 eggs, beaten
⅔ cup flour
2 squares chocolate, melted
1 teaspoon vanilla

Cream butter and sugar. Add beaten eggs, vanilla. Add sifted flour and melted chocolate. Bake in greased 8" x 8" pan 25 minutes at 325 degrees.

133

English Plum Pudding

                1 cup sugar
                2 eggs, well beaten
            ½ cup milk (about)
                1 teaspoon lemon juice
                2 cups fine dry bread crumbs
                1 cup suet, chopped fine
                2 cups raw potatoes, grated
                1 cup raw carrots, grated
                2 cups flour
                3 teaspoons baking powder
                1 teaspoon cinnamon
            ½ teaspoon nutmeg
            ½ teaspoon allspice
                1 cup currants
            1½ cups sultana raisins
            ¼ cup almonds, chopped

Blend sugar and eggs well. Add milk and lemon juice. Combine with crumbs, suet, potatoes, and carrots. Sift 1½ cups flour, baking powder, and spices together and add to mixture. Dredge fruit and nuts with ½ cup flour and add. Mix all well.

Put into 2 buttered 1 pound coffee cans with tight lids and steam 4 hours. Serve with hard sauce (flavored with rum or brandy, optional).

Green Tomato Pie

Green Tomato Pie is an old, old standby from the days when fruits were not so plentiful as they are now.

                Pastry for 2 crusts
                3 tablespoons flour
            1¼ cups sugar
            ¼ teaspoon salt
                1 tablespoon cinnamon
                3 cups peeled green tomatoes, thinly sliced
                3 tablespoons lemon juice
                1 tablespoon vinegar or lemon rind
                Dots of butter

Bake 10 minutes in hot oven (400 degrees) and 35 or 40 minutes in moderate oven (350 degrees).

RAMSEY COUNTY Minnesota's smallest, was started by settlers evicted from the Fort Snelling reservation in the 1840's. In 1843 an observer wrote that St. Paul "had but three or four log houses, and was a mixture of forests, hills, running brooks, ravines, bog mires, lakes, whisky, mosquitoes, snakes and Indians." It became the beautiful capital city.

French Salad Dressing

- 1 tablespoon sugar
- 1 teaspoon salt
- 1 teaspoon mustard
- 1 teaspoon paprika
- 1 tablespoon Worcestershire sauce
- 1 cup vinegar
- 1 cup tomato soup
- 1 cup salad oil
- 1 onion, minced
- 1 garlic, minced
- 1 green pepper, minced
- 1 cup celery, minced

Blend all ingredients thoroughly.

Hot Crab Salad

- 1 pound crab meat or shrimp
- 1 cup celery, diced
- 1 large green pepper, diced
- 1 medium-sized onion, diced
- 1 cup mayonnaise
- 2 eggs, beaten

Toss together. Place in greased scallop shells or other individual molds, sprinkle with grated cheese and bake 30 minutes at 350 degrees. Serve immediately.

Dill Soup Delicious

Peel 2 large potatoes, cut in pieces, cover with water and boil until soft. Season with salt and pepper. Don't pour off water, but mash potatoes in it. Add a cup of rich milk, heat but don't boil. Now break an egg in soup and stir. The egg will coddle and look like wisps of white and yellow lace. Wash several sprays of fresh green dill (leaves) and add to soup. Heat about 5 minutes and serve.

French Layer Cake

2 cups sugar

1 cup butter

4 yolks, well beaten

1 cup milk

3 cups flour

2 teaspoons baking powder

4 whites, well beaten

½ cup raisins, chopped

½ cup currants, chopped

½ teaspoon cinnamon

½ teaspoon nutmeg

1 teaspoon vanilla

4 teaspoons chocolate

Lemon flavoring

Cream sugar and butter, add egg yolks, well-beaten. Add milk, flour, baking powder, and lastly, well-beaten egg whites.

Divide dough into 3 parts. Add raisins, currants, cinnamon, and nutmeg to one part. Bake as one layer. Into second layer stir vanilla and chocolate. Flavor the last layer with lemon. Bake at 350 degrees, 30 to 40 minutes. Put together with chocolate frosting.

Lamb with String Beans (Lebanese)

1 pound shoulder lamb, cut up

1 clove garlic, chopped fine

1 medium-sized onion, chopped

1 large stalk celery, chopped

1 No. 2 can whole tomatoes

2 cups water

1 No. 2 can fancy cut green beans

Sauté meat with garlic, add salt and pepper. After meat is tender, add onion and cook about 5 minutes. Add celery, cook about 5 minutes, then add tomatoes and water. Cook until meat is almost done. Add beans; heat thoroughly. Serve with fluffy rice.

Rice

1¼ cups rice

4 tablespoons butter

Chicken broth or boiling water

1 cup Vermicelli (fine spaghetti), broken in small pieces

Soak rice in boiling water and salt for ½ hour or more. Drain and rinse with cold water. Melt butter, add Vermicelli, stirring constantly until very brown. Add drained rice and stir until rice becomes glossy. Add salt to taste, then add enough boiling chicken broth or water to cover. Stir until mixture begins to boil. Cover and simmer until dry. (Use heavy kettle with tight cover.)

RED LAKE COUNTY was a Christmas present to its settlers in 1896. In the late 1880's it was part of Polk county but Red Lake Falls wanted to be a county seat. Finally, in an 1896 election, propositions for five new counties were on the ballot. Three won, but they overlapped. The governor, on Christmas eve, recognized Red Lake.

Oatmeal Bread

1 cup rolled oats
2 cups boiling water
1 yeast cake
½ cup cold water
½ cup molasses
1½ teaspoons salt
1 tablespoon shortening
4 to 5 cups flour

Pour the boiling water over the oatmeal, add the shortening and cool. Add yeast, which has been dissolved in cold water, and the remaining ingredients; knead lightly. Add flour to make a stiff dough. Let rise and knead down and let rise again. Form into loaves. Bake 40 minutes in 375 degree oven.

Angel Delight

1 No. 2 can crushed pineapple
1 4-ounce box marshmallows, finely cut
1 8-ounce bottle maraschino cherries
1 envelope plain gelatin
1 cup milk
1 cup blanched almonds, chopped
1 pint heavy cream, whipped
1 10-inch (large) angel food cake

Combine pineapple, marshmallows, and cherries, including juices (save out a few cherries for decoration). Let soak 6 hours or overnight.

Soften gelatin in ½ cup cold milk 5 minutes; add ½ cup hot milk. Chill until slightly thickened. Add fruit mixture and almonds. Fold in whipped cream. Cut angel food cake into 2 layers. Put layers together with mixture and frost top and sides. If you still have mixture left, drop in middle. Chill cake before serving. Decorate with cherries and almond halves.

Krispie Bars

4 cups corn flakes
1 cup Rice Krispies
1 cup salted peanuts
1 cup coconut
1 cup cream
1 cup syrup (white)
1 cup sugar
1 teaspoon vanilla

Mix cereals, peanuts, and coconut together in large kettle. Cook cream, syrup, and sugar until it forms a soft ball in cold water. Add vanilla. Pour this mixture over the dry ingredients, put in a pan and press. Cool and cut.

Powdered Sugar Cookies

2 cups flour
1 cup powdered sugar
1 cup butter
1 teaspoon soda
1 teaspoon cream of tartar
Speck of salt
1 egg, beaten
1 teaspoon vanilla

Mix the first 6 ingredients like pie crust. Then add beaten egg and vanilla. Roll into small balls and press with a fork. If dough is too sticky, let rest in refrigerator for a few minutes. Bake at 375 degrees for 10 minutes.

Zesty Hot Dish

1½ pounds ground beef
2 large potatoes, sliced thin
1 large onion, sliced thin
1 cup uncooked rice
1 No. 2 can kidney beans
Salt and pepper
1 can tomato soup
1 can water

Take half of the above and arrange in layers in the order named. Season with salt and pepper. Repeat the process, using remainder of ingredients. Mix soup and water, pour liquid over meat and vegetables and bake covered at 350 degrees for 2 hours. Remove cover the last 20 minutes.

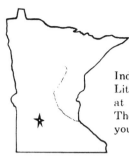

REDWOOD COUNTY was the home of four important Indian chiefs at the time of the 1862 massacre. One was Little Crow, leader of the outbreak. Later, uneasy settlers at Redwood Falls built a stockade around their town. They went out to farm in the daylight but at nightfall young and old stayed inside the stockade.

Swedish Tea Ring

½ cup scalded milk, plus 2 tablespoons
½ cup shortening, melted
   (part or all butter)
½ cup sugar
½ teaspoon salt
 1 cake compressed yeast
 2 tablespoons lukewarm water
 3 to 3½ cups all-purpose flour, sifted
 2 eggs, beaten

Combine scalded milk, shortening, sugar, and salt; cool to lukewarm. Soften yeast in lukewarm water; stir and combine with cooled milk mixture; add about half the flour; add the beaten eggs; beat well. Add enough of the remaining flour to make a soft dough; mix thoroughly.

Turn out on lightly-floured board and knead about 10 minutes or until smooth and satiny. Place dough in a warm greased bowl; brush surface very lightly with melted shortening; cover and let rise in a warm place about 2 hours or until doubled in bulk.

Now turn out on board; roll into a rectangle ¼" thick and about 8" wide. Brush with melted butter. Combine ⅔ cup brown sugar with 2 teaspoons cinnamon; spread over the dough. Roll jelly-roll fashion; shape on greased baking sheet into a ring, sealing ends together. From the outside cut through the ring toward the center almost all the way through in 1" slices. Turn slices slightly on side. Brush lightly with melted shortening; cover and let rise about ¾ hour or until doubled in bulk. Bake in a moderate oven (375 degrees) for 25 to 30 minutes.

While still warm brush with confectioner's frosting (1 cup powdered sugar, 1 tablespoon hot milk, ½ teaspoon vanilla) and then sprinkle with chopped nuts.

Two-way Seafood Salad

1 medium-sized green pepper, chopped fine
1 medium-sized onion, chopped fine or grated
1 cup celery
1 6½-ounce can crab meat
1 5¾-ounce can shrimp
½ teaspoon salt
⅛ teaspoon pepper
1 teaspoon Worcestershire sauce
½ cup mayonnaise
1 cup buttered crumbs
Parsley

Combine all ingredients except crumbs and parsley. Chill and use as a salad or place in oven and bake at 350 degrees for 30 minutes. Serve hot. Decorate in either instance with parsley and bread crumbs.

Mincemeat Coffee Cake

½ cup shortening
1 cup sugar
2 eggs
2 cups flour
2 teaspoons baking powder
¼ teaspoon salt
1 teaspoon lemon extract
1 cup milk, less 2 tablespoons
1 cup mincemeat
¼ cup walnut meats, chopped
2 tablespoons melted butter
2 tablespoons brown sugar
1 teaspoon cinnamon

Cream shortening and sugar together; stir in well-beaten eggs. Sift flour, measure, then sift again with baking powder and salt. Add lemon extract to milk and stir into creamed mixture alternately with dry ingredients.

Combine mincemeat and nuts. Spread ⅔ of batter in greased 8″ spring pan mold. Dot with ½ of the mincemeat mixture, distributing it over the batter by the teaspoonful. Cover with remaining batter and dot with rest of mincemeat. Sprinkle with melted butter, brown sugar, and cinnamon. Bake at 350 degrees for 45 minutes. Serve warm. It can also be served as a dessert with a warm lemon sauce.

RENVILLE COUNTY is named for Joseph Renville, a picturesque half-breed who had been a captain with the British forces in 1812. He built a stockade overlooking Lac qui Parle lakè in the 1820's and lived on an almost feudal scale. He asked missionaries to come to the area and helped them translate the Bible into the Sioux tongue.

Pineapple Cookies

½ cup shortening
1 cup brown sugar, firmly packed
1 egg
¾ cup crushed pineapple, drained
1 teaspoon vanilla
2 cups sifted flour
¼ teaspoon baking soda
¼ teaspoon salt
1½ teaspoons baking powder

Cream shortening; gradually add sugar, creaming well. Add egg and beat well. Add crushed pineapple and vanilla. Sift dry ingredients and add to first mixture. Drop from teaspoon about 2″ apart on greased cookie sheet. Bake at 325 degrees for about 12 minutes.

Add powdered sugar to pineapple juice to make frosting.

Cherry Torte

1 cup sifted cake flour
½ cup butter
5 tablespoons powdered sugar
2 beaten eggs
¼ teaspoon salt
¾ teaspoon baking powder
1 teaspoon vanilla
1½ cups sugar
¼ cup flour
¾ cup pecans
1 No. 2 can (20 oz.) sour cherries, drained

Mix together, like a pie crust, the cake flour, butter, and powdered sugar. Pour into bottom of 9″ square pan. Pat lightly. Bake 15 minutes at 350 degrees. Mix together remaining ingredients and pour over baked crust. Bake 30 minutes. Serve with whipped cream or vanilla ice cream.

Applesauce Bars

> 1 cup sugar
> ¾ cup shortening (some butter)
> 1 egg
> 2 cups sweetened applesauce
> 2 cups flour
> 2 teaspoons soda
> 1 cup nuts, chopped
> 1 cup dates, chopped
> ½ teaspoon cinnamon
> 1 teaspoon vanilla
> ½ teaspoon salt

Cream sugar and shortening, add beaten egg and applesauce. Sift flour, soda, salt, and spices. Add to first mixture. Add dates, nuts, and vanilla.

Bake in a moderate oven (350 degrees) for 25 minutes in an 11″ x 16″ or jelly roll pan. Spread brown sugar frosting over while hot. When cool, cut in bars.

Brown Sugar Frosting

> ¼ cup butter
> ½ cup brown sugar
> Pinch salt
> 2 tablespoons milk
> 1¼ cups powdered sugar
> ¼ teaspoon vanilla

Melt butter in pan. Stir in brown sugar, salt. Boil 2 minutes. Add milk and boil 1 minute. Remove from fire and add powdered sugar and vanilla.

Mystery Fruit Cake

For busy women who do not have time to prepare those elaborate fruit cakes, the joy of our mothers' generation, here is one which has been found very satisfactory.

Bake ½ package of yellow or white cake mix in an ordinary pan, then crumble or cut in small pieces. Now mix 2 cups of mixed, candied fruit, about 1 cup of red and green candied cherries, 1 scant cup of raisins, scant cup of cut-up dates, 2 cups of cut-up pecans. Mix all of these ingredients in a large bowl.

Now prepare ½ recipe of ready-mix frosting; when cool, add to the cake mixture and stir. Mix it very thoroughly. When well-blended, pack tightly into an 8½″ x 4½″ x 3″ pan, lined with tin foil, and smooth it compactly with buttered hands. Store it; it improves with age. Use sharp knife to cut it.

RICE COUNTY was long the headquarters of Henry Benjamin Whipple, first Episcopal bishop of the state and friend of the Indians. Faribault was the nucleus of his Indian missions. Whipple felt the Indians were badly treated and went to Washington after the Sioux uprising to plead with Lincoln for the lives of the Indian prisoners.

Hannah's Molasses Cookies

Hannah Bollenbach of Nerstrand has been baking these cookies for over 75 years. They have always been a favorite and still are with everyone in the community. Hannah's mother died when she was 8 years old, and she began to make cookies like "mother used to make" for her younger brothers and sisters. Practice makes perfect.

1⅓ cups open-kettle rendered lard
1½ cups white sugar
2 beaten eggs
1 teaspoon cinnamon
½ teaspoon nutmeg
¼ teaspoon ginger
¼ teaspoon allspice
Pinch of cloves
2⅔ cups dark molasses
1 pint rich sour cream
1⅓ cups sour milk
3 teaspoons soda
⅓ cup milk
1 teaspoon salt
1 teaspoon vanilla
1 teaspoon lemon
8 cups flour, for a very soft dough
1 teaspoon baking powder

Cream lard and sugar, add eggs, spices, molasses, sour cream, sour milk in which soda has been dissolved, salt, and flavorings. Add flour and baking powder. It's very important to keep dough very soft so use no more flour than necessary. Bake at 350 degrees until cookies puff up and spring back like a cake. Place a raisin in the center of each cookie before baking.

Fried Pies

This is an old New England recipe which few people know of these days. Dried apples were probably used because of a lack of fresh ones. This recipe is given by Miss Martha Watts of Northfield who was 101 years old February 23, 1958.

Make doughnut dough. Roll out. Cut into medium-sized circles. Place in center of each a spoonful or two of cooked and drained dried apples. Moisten edges of circle, fold over and press firmly together. Slide into hot fat and fry as you would doughnuts.

Marshmallow Cake

2 cups cake flour
2 cups white sugar
1 cup hot water
6 egg whites, beaten
1 teaspoon cream of tartar
¼ teaspoon salt
2 teaspoons baking powder
1 teaspoon vanilla

Sift cake flour and sugar together 7 times. Add hot water and stir until smooth. Set aside to cool. Beat egg whites with cream of tartar and salt. Add baking powder and beat until very light. Combine with first mixture, folding gently. Add vanilla. Bake 40 minutes at 350 degrees.

Ground Raisin Cookies

2 cups white sugar
1 cup shortening
3 eggs
½ teaspoon salt
1 cup heavy rich sour cream
1 teaspoon cinnamon
1 teaspoon nutmeg
1 teaspoon soda
2 cups ground raisins
6 cups flour, about

Roll dough and use cookie cutters. Sprinkle sugar over dough before cutting (optional). Bake at 350 degrees until light brown. Excellent storing quality.

ROCK COUNTY takes its name from a vast bluff of quartzite, about three miles long, near the center of the county. It's known, too, as the Blue Mound and it may be that Indians used to drive herds of buffalo over it to their death below. It was in this then-wild area that the Jesse James gang hid out after their 1876 raid on the Northfield bank.

Ham Cones

1 pound cooked ham, ground
1 tablespoon onion, grated
1 tablespoon parsley, chopped
1 tablespoon prepared mustard
2 tablespoons pineapple syrup
1 egg, slightly beaten
½ cup crushed corn flakes
6 pineapple slices

Mix first 6 ingredients together thoroughly. Shape into 6 cone-shaped patties. Roll cones in corn flakes and freeze. To prepare for serving, place the ham cones on the pineapple slices in a shallow baking dish and bake at 375 degrees for 45 minutes.

Curried String Beans with Rice

2 tablespoons butter or drippings
1 teaspoon curry powder
½ cup onion, sliced
¼ cup flour
2 cups milk
1 teaspoon salt
⅛ teaspoon pepper
1 cup string beans, cooked
3 cups rice, cooked
¾ cup dry rice
1 egg, slightly beaten
¾ teaspoon salt
⅛ teaspoon pepper
2 tablespoons American cheese, grated

Melt fat and add curry powder and onion. Cook until onion is browned. Blend in flour. Add milk, 1 teaspoon salt, and ⅛ teaspoon pepper. Cook until thickened, stirring constantly. Add beans. Place bean mixture in greased 2-quart casserole. Combine rice, egg, remaining salt and pepper; spread over beans. Top with cheese. Bake at 350 degrees for 30 minutes. Serves 6.

Cream Cheese Cake

1 pound cream cheese
3 eggs
⅔ cup sugar
½ teaspoon almond extract
1 cup commercial sour cream
3 tablespoons sugar
1 teaspoon vanilla

Beat cream cheese, eggs, the ⅔ cup sugar, and almond extract together very thoroughly, or until smooth and thick and lemon-colored. Pour into greased 9" pie plate. Bake at 350 degrees for 25 minutes. Cool 20 minutes.

While cheese cake is cooling, beat sour cream, the 3 tablespoons sugar and vanilla together thoroughly. Pour sour cream mixture over top of cheese cake. Return to 350 degree oven and bake 10 minutes longer. Cool before serving. Sprinkle slivered Brazil nuts on top before serving.

Daffodil Asparagus

1 8-ounce package cream cheese
2 egg yolks
2 tablespoons lemon juice
⅛ teaspoon salt
2 pounds hot cooked asparagus

Soften cream cheese. Add egg yolks, one at a time, beating thoroughly after each addition. Add lemon juice and salt; mix thoroughly. Place in covered saucepan and heat slowly for 20 minutes. When ready to serve, turn heat to medium and cook 1 minute, stirring constantly. Serve over hot asparagus. Makes 6 servings.

Spare Rib Soup

2 to 2½ pounds spare ribs,
    cut in serving pieces
1 pound dried (large) lima beans
1 No. 2 can tomatoes
2 medium-sized potatoes, cut fine
2 carrots, diced
1 onion, cut fine
    A few celery leaves or
    2 stalks of celery (optional)
Salt and pepper

Cover well with water. Bring to a boil, then simmer for about 2 hours or until beans are soft. Serves six.

When served with hot rolls, a simple salad, lemon pie, and coffee, this makes a delicious meal.

ROSEAU COUNTY has a ghost, Windego, the ghost of Roseau lake. It "lives" near Ross and for generations terrified Indians in the area. To them, sight of it meant death. A white settler, Jesse Nelson, wrote vividly of seeing it, too—"about fifteen feet tall, dressed in some material that looked like white lace." An Indian died the next morning.

Apple Custard

8 large firm apples
½ cup sugar
2 tablespoons butter
⅓ cup water
3 eggs, beaten slightly
1 cup milk
3 tablespoons sugar
⅛ teaspoon salt
3 tablespoons flour

Peel and cut apples into eighths. Cook in syrup made of sugar, butter, and water. Pour into buttered casserole and cool. Make a custard of remaining ingredients and pour over apples.

Bake in a slow oven (250 degrees) until custard is set. Serve with or without whipped cream on top.

Herring Salad

3 pounds gaffelbiter, diced
2 cups cooked veal, diced
5 medium-sized potatoes, boiled and diced
3 tart apples (with skins), diced
2 cans (4 cups) beets, diced
1 onion, minced
3 stalks celery, diced

Toss all together, add dressing and garnish with hard-cooked eggs.

Dressing

2 hard-boiled eggs, mashed
½ teaspoon salt
¼ teaspoon pepper
2 raw eggs, beaten
½ teaspoon dry mustard
1 tablespoon sugar
4 tablespoons vinegar

Swedish Heirloom Cookies

Mrs. Edward Russell, early resident of Baudette and Warroad, still uses this recipe which she received from her grandmother in Sweden. Her daughter, Mrs. Carlos Wheaton, of Hopkins, won honorable mention with this recipe at the Pillsbury National Bake-off a few years ago.

> 1 cup butter
> 1 tablespoon vanilla
> 1 cup confectioner's sugar
> ¼ teaspoon salt
> 1¼ cups almonds, ground
> 2 cups sifted flour

Cream butter, vanilla, sugar, and salt. Add almonds. Blend in flour. Shape dough into "britches" (an upside down U-shape). Bake on ungreased cookie sheet in a slow (325 degree) oven for 15 to 18 minutes. Roll in confectioner's sugar while warm.

Vineterte Cake (Icelandic)

Prepare prune filling (Sveskumauk) as follows:
Simmer 2 pounds prunes with moderate amount of water until very well done. Cool. Save liquid, remove pits, and mash or grind prunes (can use beater). Add 1 cup sugar, ½ cup prune liquid, and if desired ½ teaspoon cardamom seeds. Bring to boil in a heavy pan over low heat. Remove from fire, and when cool add ¼ teaspoon salt and 1 teaspoon vanilla.
While the filling cools, prepare dough as follows:

> 1 cup butter
> 1 cup sugar
> 2 eggs, beaten slightly
> 1 teaspoon vanilla
> 4 cups sifted flour
> 2 teaspoons baking powder
> ½ teaspoon salt
> ¼ cup milk

Cream butter and sugar; add eggs and vanilla. Sift flour, baking powder, and salt together. Add alternately to creamed mixture with milk.
Chill dough; then divide dough into 7 portions. Roll each out to fit 8″ cake pan, square or oblong preferred. Baked layers should not be more than ¼″ thick and well done. Bake in 350 degree oven about 20 minutes. Spread with filling as soon as cooled, and cure overnight or longer. Slice thin to serve.
In order to facilitate the handling of sheets of dough, identical pans should be used. Cover one with pastry cloth and roll dough over this, then lay another pan on and turn over.

ST. LOUIS COUNTY Minnesota's largest, is full of superlatives. Duluth has one of the nation's greatest harbors. At Hibbing, on the Mesabi iron range, is the biggest hole ever dug by man. North to the border is some of the wildest wilderness. And its 6,711 square miles make it twice as big as its nearest competitor in the state.

Lancaster Chicken with Cream Gravy

1 5-pound stewing chicken, cut up
Handful celery tops
3 cups water
Butter
1 teaspoon salt
1 large can evaporated milk
1 onion, chopped
½ teaspoon ginger
½ cup flour
¼ teaspoon pepper
2 tablespoons lemon juice

Simmer chicken with onion, celery tops, and ginger in water 1½ to 2 hours or just until tender. Remove chicken; strain broth and skim off fat for gravy.

Heat chicken fat with enough butter to make ½ cup in large saucepan. Remove from heat; stir in flour, salt, and pepper; gradually add broth, with water if needed, to make 3 cups. Cook, stirring constantly, until gravy thickens and boils 1 minute. Stir in evaporated milk and lemon juice. Heat to boiling. Brown cooked chicken pieces lightly in butter in fry pan. Arrange on serving platter; pour hot gravy over chicken and serve.

Tourtiere Pie

Pastry for 2 crusts
1½ pounds fresh pork, ground coarsely
1 medium-sized onion, ground fine
¼ teaspoon allspice
¼ teaspoon summer savory
¼ teaspoon sage
½ teaspoon salt
⅛ teaspoon pepper

Mix pork, onion, and spices together and put into pastry-lined pie tin. Top with the second crust and seal edges. Prick top crust and bake for 1 hour in a hot oven (400 degrees).

Liver Ball Soup (Bohemian)

2 pounds beef brisket, cubed
2 teaspoons salt
¼ teaspoon pepper
1 bay leaf
1 cup celery, coarsely chopped
1½ cups canned tomatoes
1 cup carrots, sliced

Cover brisket with cold water; add salt, pepper, and bay leaf; simmer 1 hour. Add celery, tomatoes, carrots. Simmer 1½ hours. Strain stock; force vegetables through colander. Add to meat stock. Re-heat. Add liver balls.

Liver Balls

½ pound liver, ground
¾ cup dry bread crumbs
¼ cup parsley, finely chopped
⅛ teaspoon celery seed
¼ teaspoon salt
1/16 teaspoon pepper
2 tablespoons flour
1 beaten egg
½ teaspoon onion juice

Combine all ingredients. Chill thoroughly. Form into 1″ balls; drop into hot soup. Simmer 15 minutes.

Piroki (Ukrainian)

3 cups flour
2 eggs
1 teaspoon salt
1 tablespoon soft butter

Sift flour and combine with salt, butter, and slightly-beaten eggs. Roll out thin on floured board and cut in 2″ squares. Place on each square ½ teaspoonful of filling. Fold in half to make a triangle, pinch edges securely to hold filling while cooking. Drop into boiling water for 10 minutes. Good served with plain melted butter or with 1 onion sautéed in butter.

Filling

3 potatoes, boiled and mashed
2 tablespoons butter
1 or 2 slices cheddar cheese, cubed
Salt to taste

SCOTT COUNTY, truck garden to the Twin Cities, has a breathtaking offering for sightseers. It's Lookout Point at the top of the bluffs across the Minnesota river from Shakopee. The Point commands a view of great beauty along the river in both directions. Shakopee, the county seat, is on the site of a former Indian village headed by Chief Shakpa.

Grapefruit Alaska

> 3 grapefruit, halved
> 2 teaspoons powdered sugar
> 6 teaspoons maraschino cherry syrup
> 1 pint ice cream
> 4 egg whites
> ¼ teaspoon almond extract
> ½ cup sugar

Loosen grapefruit sections, remove seeds and core. Add ½ teaspoon sugar and 1 teaspoon cherry syrup to each half. Chill thoroughly. Place a spoonful of ice cream in center, flattening the top slightly. Prepare a meringue of egg whites, almond extract, and sugar. Spread over ice cream, bringing to edge of grapefruit. Brown meringue at 500 degrees for 3 or 4 minutes. Serve immediately.

Pear Cream

> 1 tablespoon gelatin
> 2 tablespoons cold water
> 2 eggs, separated
> ¼ cup sugar
> ¼ teaspoon salt
> 2 cups scalded milk
> 2 tablespoons sugar
> 1 teaspoon vanilla
> 6 pear halves, cooked

Soften gelatin in cold water for 5 minutes. Beat egg yolks, sugar, and salt together until light. Add milk slowly to egg yolk mixture. Cook over low heat, stirring constantly, until mixture coats a spoon. Remove custard and add softened gelatin and stir until dissolved. Cool to room temperature. Beat egg whites with sugar and vanilla until mixture stands in peaks. Fold into custard. Arrange pear halves in serving dish (or individual dishes), pour custard over them. Chill until firm.

Western Salad

    1 medium-sized avocado
    2 cups grapefruit sections
    12 pitted ripe olives

Cut avocado in half, twist to loosen seed and remove peel. Cut in crosswise slices. Marinate avocado and grapefruit sections in Lemon-Lime Dressing. Arrange avocado and grapefruit on lettuce and sprinkle with chopped olives.

Lemon-Lime Dressing

    ⅓ cup lemon juice
    1½ tablespoons lime juice
    ⅔ cup salad oil
    1 teaspoon salt
    1 teaspoon paprika
    1 tablespoon sugar or honey

Caramel Apple Cake

    2 cups brown sugar
    1 cup butter (part shortening is fine)
    2 eggs, well beaten
    3 cups flour, sifted
    ½ teaspoon salt
    ½ teaspoon nutmeg
    2 teaspoons soda
    ½ cup walnuts, chopped
    1 cup dates, cut up
    1 cup strong coffee, cooled
    2 cups apples, diced

Cream brown sugar and shortening; add well-beaten eggs. Sift dry ingredients together. Blend in dates and walnuts. Add to creamed mixture alternately with coffee. Beat just until mixtures are blended. Add apples and again stir just enough to blend. Bake in 8″ x 12″ greased, lightly-floured pan at 350 degrees for 45 to 50 minutes. Frost with Caramel Frosting.

Caramel Frosting

    1 cup brown sugar, firmly packed
    3 tablespoons shortening
    2 tablespoons butter
    ¼ teaspoon salt
    ¼ cup milk
    1½ cups confectioner's sugar, sifted

Combine brown sugar, shortening, butter, salt, and milk and bring to a boil, stirring constantly. Boil 3 minutes; cool. Beat in confectioner's sugar until of spreading consistency.

SHERBURNE COUNTY has some genuine sand dunes, shifted endlessly by the winds, which seem a startling incongruity in the center of fertile Minnesota. The county seat, Elk River, and the river that joins the Mississippi here, are named for the herds of elk which Zebulon Pike found when he explored southern Minnesota.

Beef Stroganoff

                3 tablespoons flour
            1½ teaspoons salt
            ¼ teaspoon pepper
                1 pound beef tenderloin (cut ¼" thick)
                1 clove garlic
            ¼ cup butter
            ½ cup onion, chopped
            ¼ cup water
                1 cup chicken soup, undiluted
                1 pound mushrooms, sliced
                1 cup sour cream
                Parsley, chopped

Dredge meat in flour, salt, and pepper. Rub on garlic. Cut meat into strips and then brown in butter. Next saute onions; add water. Stir to dissolve brown particles in pan. Add soup and mushrooms; cook uncovered over low heat for about 20 minutes or until meat is tender. Stir in sour cream and re-heat but do not boil. Sprinkle with parsley.

Rice Pudding (Norwegian)

                4 cups water
                2 cups milk
            ½ teaspoon salt
                1 cup rice
            ½ cup sugar
            ¾ cup heavy cream
                1 teaspoon vanilla
                Pineapple, if desired

Bring water, milk, salt to boil. Add the rice and sugar. Cook over low heat for 30 minutes, or until rice is soft and fluffy. Stir gently once or twice. Chill. Whip the cream, add vanilla and mix with rice just before serving. Pineapple may be added.

Seafood Casserole

                2 slices bacon, diced
                1 clove garlic, minced
                2 medium-sized onions, sliced
                1 cup celery, diced
                ½ cup shredded green pepper
                1 teaspoon chili powder
                1 No. 2 can tomatoes
                ¾ cup Minute Rice
            1½ cups water
                1 tablespoon vinegar
                ½ cup green peas (cooked)
                1 teaspoon sugar
                ½ pound shrimp, cooked
                12 oysters

Sauté the bacon; add garlic, onion, celery, pepper, bay leaf.
Cook slowly until tender. Add chili, pepper, tomatoes, water, rice,
vinegar, and sugar. Bring to a boil. Pour into casserole. Cover and
bake at 375 degrees for 45 minutes. Add peas, shrimp, and oysters.
Mix in lightly. Return to oven uncovered about 10 minutes longer
or until oysters are done. Serve at once. Makes 6 to 8 servings.

English Toffee

                1 cup crushed vanilla wafers
                3 eggs, separated
                1 cup walnuts, chopped
                1 cup powdered sugar
                ¼ pound butter
            1½ squares bitter chocolate, melted
                ½ teaspoon vanilla
                Whipping cream

Roll vanilla wafers into crumbs and mix together with chopped
nuts. Using half of the mixture, cover the bottom of a buttered
9″ x 9″ pan. Cream butter and sugar; add beaten egg yolks, melted
chocolate, and vanilla. Fold in beaten whites. Pour over wafers
and spread remaining crumbs on top. Put in refrigerator overnight.
Cut in squares and serve with whipped cream. Serves 6.

SIBLEY COUNTY named for the first governor of the state, followed the lead of Joseph R. Brown, one of the state's key pioneers. Brown planned to build a road west across the county. He started the town of Henderson and settlers came fast to claim the fertile new soil. The first house in the county was built mostly of hay.

Apple Cake (Dutch)

> 2 cups flour
> 3 teaspoons baking powder
> ½ teaspoon salt
> 2 tablespoons shortening
> 3/5 cup milk
> 2 tablespoons sugar
> Apples
> 1 cup sugar

Mix all ingredients except the cream, sugar, and apples. Put in pan 10″ x 15″. Peel apples, slice; arrange apple slices across cake. Put ½ cup cream on apples. Sprinkle 1 cup sugar and a little cinnamon on too. Bake about 20 minutes at 375 degrees.

Sauerbraten

> 3 pounds pot roast of beef
> 1 cup cider vinegar
> 1 cup water
> 3 bay leaves
> 4 cloves
> 2 teaspoons salt
> Pepper to taste

Bring vinegar, water, and spices to the boiling point, then pour over the meat which has been placed in a narrow bowl deep enough so the vinegar mixture will cover it. Set aside in a cool place for 4 or 5 days, turning meat occasionally.

Remove meat from vinegar and brown in fat. Then add vinegar mixture and a little more water and simmer about 3 hours. Add onions and carrots for flavor the last hour of baking. Add water as needed. Thicken gravy. Sweet cream added about ½ hour before serving improves the flavor.

Chicken Almond Casserole

1 cup long-grain rice
2 tablespoons fat

Brown rice in hot fat, stirring constantly. This takes about 5 minutes. Then cook the rice, covered, in water for 10 to 15 minutes or until rice is almost tender. Drain off water.

2 tablespoons butter, melted
2 tablespoons flour
1 14½-ounce can evaporated milk
1 cup chicken broth (or dissolve 1 chicken bouillon cube in 1 cup water)
1¼ teaspoons salt
1 tablespoon Worcestershire sauce
1½ cups cooked or canned chicken, diced
1 3-ounce can mushrooms, drained and sliced
⅓ cup pimiento, chopped
⅓ cup green pepper, chopped
½ cup blanched almonds, slivered

Blend butter and flour together in saucepan. Stir in the milk and broth and cook until thick. Stir constantly. Add all of remaining ingredients plus the already-prepared rice. Place in a 2-quart casserole. Toss bread crumbs in 2 tablespoons of butter; sprinkle over top.

Bake at 350 degrees for 25 minutes. Garnish with parsley.

Steak Hot Dish

1½ pounds round steak, cut into serving pieces
2 tablespoons flour
½ teaspoon paprika
½ teaspoon salt
¼ teaspoon pepper
2 tablespoons shortening
1 No. 2 can tomatoes
½ cup uncooked rice
2 medium-sized onions, sliced thin

Dredge steak in mixture of flour, paprika, salt, and pepper; brown in shortening. Place browned steak in casserole. Make a gravy from leftover flour mixture plus ½ cup hot water. Pour over steak and then add tomatoes, rice and top with sliced onions. Bake 1 hour at 350 degrees. Serves 6.

STEARNS COUNTY and its seat, St. Cloud, have long been a Minnesota crossroads. The old trail of the Red River oxcarts met the Mississippi here and it was a campsite for the drivers. The first stagecoach line came through in 1851 and the railroad in 1866. It was an outfitting post for the fur traders, and river steamboats picked up tons of fur pelts.

Barbecued Duck

2 large duck breasts
4 teaspoons lemon juice
1 teaspoon Worcestershire sauce
1 teaspoon tomato catsup
1 tablespoon butter
1 teaspoon salt
¼ teaspoon paprika

Broil until brown or about 10 minutes. Baste frequently with barbecue sauce made of remaining ingredients. When meat begins to brown, sprinkle with salt and paprika. Continue to broil for 20 minutes or until done.

Sesame Cookies

2 beaten egg whites
1 cup sugar
1 pound dates, cut up
1 pound Turkish Delight (or gumdrops)
½ pound walnuts
½ cup coconut

Mix and roll into batter. Roll in washed and dried sesame seed. Drop on cookie sheet and bake at 350 degrees for 15 minutes.

Oil and Vinegar Dressing

2 cups olive or vegetable oil
2 scant cups sugar
1 cup vinegar
1 tablespoon salt
1 tablespoon celery salt
3 tablespoons paprika

Mix all of these ingredients with an electric mixer for 20 minutes. Then bottle. Use on any kind of salad.

Chicken Supreme

6 cups chicken, cut in pieces
3 cups cooked rice
4 cups chicken broth
3 cups milk
4 tablespoons butter
1 teaspoon salt
¾ cup flour
1 cup blanched almonds, slivered
1 small can pimiento
⅛ teaspoon pepper
1 can mushroom soup

Pour 1 cup broth over rice. Make a rich gravy by adding 3 cups broth to milk. Add flour and butter. Pat layer of rice into two 9" casseroles. Add layer of chicken, then layer of rice; add gravy and cover with buttered crumbs. Bake 30 minutes at 350 degrees.

Cheese Sandwich Spread

1 pound cream cheese
1 10-ounce bottle pimiento olives
1 onion, size of egg
1 cup nutmeats

Put cream cheese through grinder, mixed with cream until soft enough to spread. Cut all ingredients fine and add to cheese.

Oat Cakes

The first men to discover and work in the granite quarries in the St. Cloud area were Scotchmen. They had their favorite foods. One was crisp oat cakes. The following recipe was given by the American-born wife of a Scotch immigrant. Mrs. George Lehrke, St. Cloud.

4 cups oatmeal
1 scant cup flour
1 teaspoon salt
1½ teaspoons baking powder
1 cup warm water
1 heaping tablespoon lard

Mix and roll out very thin. Cut with cookie cutter. Bake in moderate oven (350 degrees).

STEELE COUNTY became Minnesota's first health resort when Chief Wadena moved his entire village so his frail daughter might drink from the mineral springs near the present Owatonna. Owatonna, which means "straight," is on the Straight river, an ironical name for a stream that stops zigging only long enough to zag.

Donna's Cole Slaw

1 large head cabbage
1 carrot
½ green pepper
2 stalks celery
1 apple

Shred all ingredients; toss with dressing and serve.

Dressing
1 cup white vinegar
1 cup sugar
2 teaspoons celery seed
2 teaspoons mustard seed

Cook 5 minutes and let stand overnight.

Ice Water Pastry

2¼ cups sifted cake flour
¾ teaspoon salt
¾ cup shortening
Ice water

Sift flour and salt together. Prepare ice water, putting several ice cubes in cold water. Fill a standard measuring cup with this ice water to ¼ mark; then fill cup with shortening until water is raised to 1 cup mark. Pour off water, then cut shortening left in cup into flour mixture with either a pastry blender or 2 knives until the flour-fat particles are about the size of navy beans. Then add 6 to 8 tablespoons of ice water, sprinkling a small portion at a time over flour-fat mixture and cutting it in with a spatula or knife. The ball of dough should be easy to handle, neither sticky because of too much water nor crumbly because of too little.

Makes two 9" pie shells.

Lemon Walnut Layers

1½ cups sugar
½ cup butter
2½ cups cake flour, sifted
½ teaspoon salt
½ cup water
1 cup whipping cream
1 cup walnut meats
1 teaspoon vanilla
3 teaspoons baking powder
½ cup milk
4 egg whites

Spread sugar and nut meats on waxed paper; crush well with rolling pin. Place in bowl with butter and flavoring. Beat with electric or rotary beater until light and fluffy. Add sifted dry ingredients alternately with combined milk and water, beating until smooth. Fold in egg whites beaten until stiff but not dry. Pour batter into 2 well-greased and floured 8″ cake pans. Bake in a moderate oven (350 degrees) 30 minutes.

Remove layers from pans; cool on cake racks. Spread half of cooled lemon custard filling between layers. Beat whipping cream until stiff; sweeten with sugar. Spread on sides of cake and about 1″ around rim. Sprinkle coarsely-grated lemon rind on the cream. Fill center with rest of filling. Chill several hours before serving.

Lemon Custard Filling

1⅓ cups sugar
4 tablespoons cornstarch
4 egg yolks
4 tablespoons lemon juice (fresh,
    frozen or canned)
1¼ cups water

Combine all ingredients in saucepan; place over heat and bring to a boil, stirring constantly. Cook 1 minute; remove from heat and stir in 1 teaspoon grated lemon rind and 1 tablespoon butter. Cool.

Whipped Cream Topping

1 cup whipping cream
½ cup sifted powdered sugar
½ teaspoon vanilla extract

Whip chilled cream, gradually adding sugar and extract until cream is thick enough to hold shape.

STEVENS COUNTY reflects the influence of the railroads that brought pioneers to the new area. The county is named for Isaac Stevens, an engineer who headed a railroad-surveying commission. Morris, the county seat, was named for a St. Paul Pacific Railway engineer who personally tacked up the sign on the railway station.

Orange Ginger Ale Ring

1 envelope gelatin
¼ cup lemon juice
¼ cup sugar
¾ cup orange juice
¼ teaspoon salt
1 cup ginger ale
1 cup orange sections
½ cup pecan halves

Soften the gelatin in the lemon juice for about 5 minutes; heat mixture until gelatin is thoroughly dissolved. Add sugar, salt, orange juice, and ginger ale. Alternate orange sections and pecan halves in the bottom of a mold. Add remaining orange sections and pecans to the gelatin mixture. Pour into mold and place in refrigerator. When ready to use, unmold, fill center with cottage cheese and garnish with orange sections. Serve with honey dressing.

Honey Dressing

⅓ cup sugar
1 teaspoon dry mustard
1 teaspoon paprika
1 teaspoon celery seed
¼ teaspoon salt
⅓ cup strained honey
5 tablespoons vinegar
1 tablespoon lemon juice
1 cup salad oil
1 teaspoon onion, grated

Mix dry ingredients. Add honey, vinegar, lemon juice, and onion. Pour oil into mixture very slowly, beating constantly with rotary or electric mixer. Makes 2 cups.

Fruit Cocktail Dessert

1 cup flour
1 cup sugar
1 teaspoon soda
¼ teaspoon salt
1 egg, beaten
1 No. 2 can fruit cocktail, drained
½ cup brown sugar
½ cup chopped nuts

Mix flour, sugar, soda, and salt; add beaten egg and drained fruit cocktail. Put into greased 6" x 8" pan; sprinkle brown sugar and nuts on top. Bake 1 hour at 325 degrees.

Russian Salad

½ pint herring (remove wine sauce)
1 cup diced beets, drained
1 cup apple, chopped
1 teaspoon onion, minced
1 dill pickle, chopped
1 teaspoon vinegar
1 tablespoon cooking oil
Pepper to suit
1 cup sour cream

Add all ingredients together. Chill and serve.

Date-filled Cookies

2 cups brown sugar
1 cup shortening
3 eggs, beaten
1 teaspoon vanilla
1 teaspoon soda in 1 tablespoon hot water
3 cups flour
A little salt

Slice when chilled or form dough with hands and put in the filling.

Date Filling

1 pound dates
½ cup sugar
1 cup water

Boil and cool.

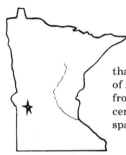

SWIFT COUNTY includes a small settlement, Clontarf, that was started in 1876 through the colonization efforts of Archbishop Ireland. He wanted to bring Irish Catholics from the "poverty stricken and demoralized crowded centers of the east" to the "wide open opportunity-waiting spaces of the west." A group from Pennsylvania did come.

Ham and Bean Soup

        1 pound dried black or kidney beans
    12 cups water
        1 meaty ham bone
        1 large onion, chopped
            Handful celery tops
        6 whole cloves
        1 bay leaf
        1 tablespoon lemon juice
        1 teaspoon Worcestershire sauce
    2½ cups ham, cubed
        2 hard-cooked eggs

Heat beans in water to boiling in large kettle. Let stand 1 hour; add ham bone, onion, celery tops, cloves, bay leaf, lemon, and Worcestershire sauce. Simmer 2 hours or until beans are tender. Remove ham bone and cube its meat; put bean mixture through food mill and re-heat to boiling. Garnish with cubed ham and hard-cooked eggs, sliced.

Jambalaya

        1 pound ham, cut in cubes
        1 tablespoon melted butter
        1 medium-sized onion, chopped
        1 medium-sized green pepper, chopped
        1 clove garlic, minced
        1 No. 2 can tomatoes
    ⅛ teaspoon Tabasco sauce
        1 cup water
        1 cup uncooked rice

Brown ham lightly in butter in a heavy pan which has a tight-fitting lid. Add onion, green pepper, and garlic. Cook 5 minutes, stirring occasionally. Blend in tomatoes, Tabasco, and water. Add rice, cover tightly. Simmer 30 minutes or until rice is done. Do not stir, but lift with fork occasionally.

Brown Rice

1 cup rice
1 small onion, minced
Tiny bit garlic, minced
2 tablespoons butter
Consomme

Brown ingredients in butter. Over them, pour 1 can of consomme plus 1 can of water. Cover and bake in moderate oven (350 degrees) for 40 minutes or in covered frying pan on top of stove.

Angel Pie

4 egg whites
1 teaspoon vinegar
1 teaspoon vanilla
1 cup sugar
½ cup chopped English walnuts or pecans
½ cup coconut
1 teaspoon baking powder
10 graham crackers, rolled fine

Beat egg whites stiff, add vinegar, vanilla; fold in sugar. Mix dry ingredients, then add egg whites; mix well. Pour into buttered pan and bake at 350 degrees about 30 minutes. Serve ice cream on top. Very tasty and rich.

Carrot and Rice Casserole

½ cup raw rice
2 cups carrots, chopped and cooked
¼ cup granulated sugar
½ teaspoon salt
2 eggs, beaten
4 cups milk

Boil rice in water until soft. Mix with other ingredients. Put into greased casserole. Bake in 350 degree oven until knife inserted in middle comes out clean. Stir once or twice when it begins to thicken.

Sauerkraut with Apples

Put 2 pounds of sauerkraut in an earthenware casserole; add 4 tablespoons of pork fat, a few tablespoons of water, 3 or 4 apples (peeled, cored, and quartered), 1 slice of onion. Cover the casserole. Cook on a brisk fire until the sauerkraut and apples are tender, then add a little salt, sugar, and a sprinkling of caraway seed and two finely-grated potatoes. Cook a few minutes longer.

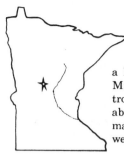

TODD COUNTY'S seat, Long Prairie, is on the site of a large community that had disappeared by the time Minnesota became a state. Indian agents moved some troublesome Winnebagoes to the area in 1846 and put up about 150 agency buildings. But the Indians went on making trouble, were moved again, and the buildings were removed by 1855.

Cherry Salad

> 1 package marshmallows, cut up
> 1 small bottle maraschino cherries
> 1 small can crushed pineapple, drained
> 1 tablespoon flour
> 1 tablespoon sugar
> 1 teaspoon butter
> 1 pint cream, whipped

Drain cherries and cut in small pieces. Mix cherries, cherry juice, and cut marshmallows and let soak 1 hour.

Cook pineapple juice, flour, sugar, and butter until thickened. Combine whipped cream, marshmallow mixture, pineapple, and cooked mixture. Chill several hours. Serve on lettuce; also makes very attractive ring mold.

Glazed Fresh Strawberry Pie

> Baked, cooled pie shell
> 1½ quarts strawberries
> ½ cup water
> 1 cup sugar
> 2½ tablespoons cornstarch
> 1 tablespoon butter
> Red food coloring

Place 1 quart of berries in baked, cooled pie shell. Crush 1 pint of strawberries and combine with water, sugar, and cornstarch in saucepan. Boil about 2 minutes or until clear. Add butter and food coloring. Spoon strawberry glaze over whole berries, making sure all berries are covered. Cool in refrigerator and serve with whipped cream.

Pound Cake

> 1 pound butter
> 1 pound sugar
> 1 pound eggs (6 to 8)
> 1 pound cake flour
> ½ teaspoon nutmeg
> 1 teaspoon vanilla

Cream butter and sugar. Beat eggs well and add. Sift cake flour with nutmeg. Add vanilla. Beat well. Put into 2 loaf pans. Bake at 325 degrees for 1 hour.

Swedish Pancakes

> 4 eggs, beaten thick
> 4 tablespoons sugar
> 4 tablespoons melted butter
> 2 cups milk
> 1 cup flour
> 2 teaspoons baking powder
> 1 teaspoon salt

Beat until smooth. Bake on a greased, heated skillet. Pour batter, tilt to spread thin, cook 1 minute until delicate brown. Loosen with spatula and flip. Serve with plain or whipped cream and fresh or frozen berries.

Bacon Corn Muffins

> 1 cup corn meal
> 1 cup sifted flour
> 1 teaspoon baking powder
> 1 teaspoon salt
> ¾ teaspoon soda
> 2 eggs, well beaten
> 2 tablespoons brown sugar
> 1½ cups sour milk
> ¼ cup diced bacon, browned

Mix all together only until smooth. Fill well-greased muffin tins ⅔ full. Bake at 425 degrees for 15 to 20 minutes.

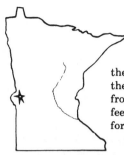

TRAVERSE COUNTY borders Lake Traverse, scene of the state's most thrilling spectacle of bird migration— the annual stopover of the blue geese. On their long flight from the Gulf of Mexico to the Arctic, they stop here to feed at night. At dawn, great flocks rise and wheel into formation—wave after wave of symmetrical V's.

Rhubarb Upside Down Cake

5 cups rhubarb
1 cup sugar
18 marshmallows, cut small

Grease large pan generously with butter. Combine ingredients and pour over this any good cake recipe or box cake mix.

Maplenut Cake Squares

4 tablespoons shortening
½ cup sugar
⅓ cup maple syrup or honey
2 eggs, beaten
1 cup flour
¼ teaspoon salt
1 teaspoon baking powder
½ cup nuts
2 to 4 tablespoons cream or milk

Cream shortening and sugar. Add the rest of the ingredients and beat 2 minutes. Pour into a shallow 9″ pan. Bake 25 minutes at 350 degrees. Cut in squares and roll in powdered sugar.

Beet Greens (European style)

Cook the greens in slightly-salted water until the stems are tender. Drain until very dry. Measure and for 2 cups of cooked beet greens, allow 2 slices of bacon and 1 egg.

Fry the bacon until quite crisp and crumble. Add the greens, heat through.

Break the egg over the greens, distribute through the greens by stirring and folding; when the egg becomes solid, remove from heat. Serve at once.

Sweet Potatoes DeLuxe

                    1 can sweet potatoes
                    1 can applesauce
                    ¼ teaspoon nutmeg
                    2 tablespoons butter
                    2 tablespoons nuts, chopped

Blend applesauce and nutmeg; arrange layer of sliced sweet potatoes in bottom of buttered baking dish. Dot with half of butter and add applesauce. Top with remaining sweet potatoes. Dot with butter and sprinkle with chopped nuts. Bake at 350 degrees 25 to 30 minutes.

Macaroon Pie

                    3 egg whites
                    ¾ cup sugar
                    20 crackers, rolled (salted, white)
                    1 teaspoon baking powder
                    ½ teaspoon vanilla
                    ½ teaspoon almond extract
                    ½ cup walnuts, chopped

Beat whites and add sugar gradually. Fold in cracker crumbs to which baking powder and nuts have been added. Bake at 350 degrees for exactly 30 minutes in a greased pie tin. Do not over-bake. Serve with whipped cream and frozen strawberries or straw-berry jam. Ice cream or custard sauce is also good.

Frosty Fruit Salad

                    ¾ cup sugar
                    1 envelope unflavored gelatin
                    ¼ cup water
                    1 egg white, stiffly beaten
                    1 cup heavy cream, whipped
                    ¼ cup salad dressing or mayonnaise
                    1 can pineapple tidbits, drained
                    1 can seedless grapes, drained
                    ½ cup broken walnut meats
                    1 can mandarin oranges, drained
                    1 cup small marshmallows

Combine sugar and gelatin; add water. Bring to a boil, then remove immediately from heat and pour over stiff egg white. Beat until thick and let cool. Add other ingredients. Pour into mold and chill.

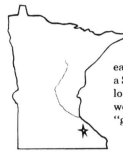

WABASHA COUNTY borders Lake Pepin, which once earned another name from Father Louis Hennepin, then a Sioux captive. A chief named Aquipaguetin would weep loudly over the bones of a dead relative until the French would bribe him to stop. There was so much of this "grief" on the trip the friar called Pepin "Lake of Tears."

Date Pinwheel Cookies

2 cups brown sugar
½ cup butter
½ cup lard
2 eggs, beaten
1 teaspoon soda, dissolved in
   1 tablespoon water
½ teaspoon salt
1 teaspoon vanilla
3½ cups flour

Mix in order given and roll out about ⅛" or ¼" thick, using an additional ½ cup flour. Spread the following date filling over the dough and roll like jelly roll. Put in the ice box to cool, then slice and bake in a moderate oven (350 degrees).

Date Filling

1 pound dates, chopped
¾ cup water
½ cup sugar
½ teaspoon vanilla

Boil until thick, remove from stove and cool. Add vanilla. A little grated orange rind in the dates gives a nice variety.

Pecan Clusters

½ cup butter
1 cup white sugar
1 egg, beaten
2 squares melted chocolate, cooled
3 teaspoons vanilla
1 cup sifted flour
½ teaspoon baking powder
1 teaspoon salt
2 cups whole pecans

Bake at 350 degrees for 10 minutes.

Pfeffernuesse

1 cup dark molasses
1 cup dark syrup
2 cups sugar
2 cups shortening
6 eggs
½ teaspoon pepper
3 teaspoons ground cardamom
2 teaspoons ground anise
2 teaspoons soda
Flour to make stiff dough

Let stand overnight. Take a portion of dough and roll it into a roll about ¾" in diameter and cut it into 1" lengths. Place these cut-side down on a cookie sheet and bake at 350 degrees.

Fresh Raspberry Pie

1 baked pastry shell, cooled
2⅔ cups fresh raspberries
⅓ cup water
⅔ cup sugar
2 tablespoons cornstarch

Wash, drain, and dry berries thoroughly. Take 1⅓ cups of fresh raspberries, add water and cook until soft. Strain through sieve. To this mixture add sugar and cornstarch. Cook until slightly thickened.

Place remaining dry berries in baked pie shell and dribble the cooked mixture over them to give a glaze. Place pie in refrigerator for 2 hours or longer to chill. Remove 15 minutes before serving and garnish with whipped cream.

Green Goddess Salad Dressing

1 clove garlic, grated
1 small can anchovies
1 tablespoon green chives, chopped
1 tablespoon lemon juice
3 tablespoons tarragon vinegar
⅛ tablespoon parsley, chopped
Salt and pepper
1 cup mayonnaise
½ cup heavy cream

Beat all ingredients together with electric beater.

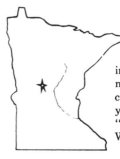

WADENA COUNTY'S "courthouse" once was a room in a private home. The commissioners rented it for $6 a month. When the home burned early in the 1880's, the county built a one-room log cabin that was used for many years. Verndale wanted to be county seat and hired "residents" at election time. So did Wadena and Wadena won.

Prize-winning Doughnuts

¾ cup milk, scalded
¼ cup melted butter
½ teaspoon vanilla
½ teaspoon lemon flavoring
½ cup egg yolks
1 cup sugar
4 cups flour, sifted
½ teaspoon salt
4 teaspoons baking powder

Scald milk, add butter and cool slightly. Beat egg yolks until thick and lemon-colored; add sugar gradually, beat until glossy; add flavoring, add milk gradually mixing well after each addition. Fold in sifted dry ingredients, blending well. Roll on lightly-floured surface to ½" thickness. Cut with doughnut cutter and fry in hot deep lard at 375 degrees. Drain on paper.

Scotch Shortbread

1 cup butter
1 cup lard
2 cups pastry flour
2½ cups all-purpose flour
½ teaspoon salt
1½ cups sugar
1 teaspoon baking powder

Cream shortening, add sugar gradually. Sift flours, baking powder, salt together and add gradually to creamed mixture. Put mixture out on board and knead like bread for 5 minutes. Pat over a cookie sheet ½" thick. Sprinkle lightly with white sugar. Bake 1 hour at 300 degrees. (It should be just a very light tan when completed.) Break into cookie-sized pieces when still warm.

Quick Hot Milk Cake

This is a summer favorite with fresh strawberries for a fast treat for drop-by guests on Sundays at the lake. Mrs. Harold Hanson, Wadena.

4 eggs, beaten
2 cups white sugar
2 cups flour
2 teaspoons baking powder
1 cup hot milk
1 tablespoon butter in the milk
1 teaspoon vanilla

Mix in order given and bake at 375 degrees in 9″ x 13″ greased pan for 25 minutes or in 3″ x 9″ greased layer pans for 20 minutes.

Tuna Salad Coneys

1 cup American cheese, cubed
3 hard-boiled eggs, chopped
1 7-ounce can tuna fish
2 tablespoons green pepper, chopped
2 tablespoons onion, chopped
2 tablespoons stuffed olives, chopped
2 tablespoons sweet pickle, chopped
½ cup mayonnaise
10 wiener buns, buttered

Lightly mix all salad ingredients. Fill the buns, wrap in tin foil. Heat on a cookie sheet at 250 degrees for 30 minutes.

Wild Rice and Tuna Casserole

1 cup unwashed wild rice
1 can tuna fish
1 can mushroom soup
1 can milk
1 small can mushrooms

Cook wild rice according to directions for cooking wild rice until fluffy. Add tuna fish, mushroom soup diluted with milk and heated. Add mushrooms that have been sautéed in butter. Bake at 300 degrees for 40 minutes.

WASECA COUNTY has a still-existing organization called the Waseca County Anti-Horse Thief Detective society. It was started in 1864, when horses were apt to be spirited away to southern battlefields. The society's members never lost a horse. These days the horseless carriage comes within its protection too.

Tomato Soup Chiffon Cake

2¼ cups sifted cake flour
1½ cups sugar
3 teaspoons baking powder
1 teaspoon salt
1 teaspoon cinnamon
½ teaspoon cloves
½ teaspoon nutmeg
1 can condensed tomato soup
½ cup salad oil
7 eggs, separated
2 teaspoons lemon rind, grated
½ teaspoon cream of tartar

Sift flour, sugar, baking powder, salt, and spices. Make a well and add in order: Soup, oil, egg yolks, and lemon rind. Beat until smooth. Beat egg whites and cream of tartar until very stiff. Gently fold first mixture into whites until just blended. Pour in ungreased 10" tube pan.

Bake at 325 degrees for 55 minutes. Then increase temperature to 350 degrees and bake 10 to 15 minutes more or until top springs back to a light touch. Remove from oven. Invert until cold. Frost if desired (lemon icing especially good).

Ina's Cheese Ball

1 pound Philadelphia cream cheese
4 ounces bleu cheese
2 teaspoons Worcestershire sauce
½ teaspoon Tabasco sauce
½ clove garlic, crushed
¼ pound Brazil nuts, shaved paper thin

Have cheeses at room temperature. Combine all ingredients except the nuts with a mixer on low speed. Wrap in waxed paper and chill. When firm, form in a ball and roll in the shaved nuts.

Place on a large cheese plate surrounded with crackers and have spreaders handy for guests to help themselves.

Tutti-frutti Cake

½ cup shortening
1 cup sugar
2 eggs, beaten
½ cup cold coffee
2 teaspoons cocoa
1 teaspoon cinnamon
½ teaspoon cloves
1 cup dates, chopped
1 cup nuts
1 cup raw peeled apples, chopped fine
1¾ cups cake flour
1 teaspoon soda
¼ teaspoon salt

Cream shortening and sugar until fluffy. Beat in the eggs. Sift flour, salt, soda, spices, and cocoa together; add alternately with the coffee. Add dates, nuts, and apples.

Bake at 350 degrees for about 30 minutes or until done. Frost with a white icing.

Cranberry Bread

2 cups flour
½ teaspoon salt
½ teaspoon soda
¾ cup sugar
1½ teaspoons baking powder
1 egg
2 tablespoons melted shortening
½ cup orange juice
2 tablespoons hot water
½ cup nuts, chopped
1 cup cranberries, chopped

Sift dry ingredients, add to liquid ingredients. Mix only until dry ingredients are blended. Fold in fruit and nuts. Pour into loaf pan and bake at 350 degrees for 1 hour and 10 minutes.

WASHINGTON COUNTY made logging history. Three miles northeast of historic Stillwater was the St. Croix boom site, where millions of logs were annually gathered, sorted, rafted, and floated to the mills. More logs—more than two million carloads of them—passed this point than passed any other one place in the nation.

Potato Cake

    ½ cup butter
    2 cups white sugar
    4 eggs
    1 cup sour milk or buttermilk
    1 cup mashed potatoes
    1 teaspoon soda
    1 teaspoon salt
    1 teaspoon vanilla
    2 cups sifted flour
    1 cup raisins
    1 cup bitter chocolate, grated
    ½ cup walnut meats

Cream butter and sugar, add mashed potatoes and beat well; add eggs and beat well. Add soda to sour milk. Sift flour and salt and add alternately with sour milk. Add raisins, vanilla, and nuts. Fold in bitter chocolate. Bake at 350 degrees in a large oblong cake pan until cake leaves the sides of pan. Frost with caramel frosting.

Angel Cookies

    4 egg whites
    2 cups powdered sugar
    2 cups dates and nut meats
    Pinch of salt
    May add a few drops of extract for flavor

Beat egg whites 3 minutes at high speed. Add sugar, mix for 10 minutes at medium speed. Fold in nuts and dates. Drop from spoon; bake 20 minutes at 325 degrees.

May add 1 cup shredded coconut.

The Famous Boom Cookies

On the St. Croix River approximately two miles north of Stillwater, early logging industries, which floated logs down the river, had a sorting and marking ground that was known as "The Boom." They employed many lumberjacks and had a cook shack at this site. These cookies were a treat to any boys who stopped at the shack at meal time. The cookies were cut with a cutter about five inches in diameter. They never seemed too large to the boys. Mrs. Albert E. Ponath, Stillwater.

1 cup sugar
1 cup lard (¾ cup butter preferred)
½ cup molasses
2 egg yolks
½ cup boiling coffee
½ teaspoon ginger
2 teaspoons soda
3 cups flour

Mix sugar, lard, and molasses. Add egg yolks. Mix coffee, ginger, and soda; add to first mixture. Add flour, roll and cut. Bake at 350 degrees.

Angel Lemon Pie

4 eggs, separated
1 teaspoon cream of tartar
1½ cups sugar
1 lemon, juice and rind
1 cup whipping cream
¼ teaspoon salt

Beat egg whites until foamy; add cream of tartar and beat until stiff but not dry. Add 1 cup sugar gradually. Put this mixture into a buttered and floured pie tin and bake at 270 degrees for 1 hour. Cool.

Now beat egg yolks until light; add juice and grated lemon rind and ½ cup sugar. Cook in double boiler until thick. Cool.

Whip cream; add 1 tablespoon sugar. Put half of the whipped cream on the cooled meringue crust; add the cooled lemon mixture, then the rest of the whipped cream. Coconut may also be sprinkled on top.

This dessert should be made about 24 hours before serving. Keep in refrigerator.

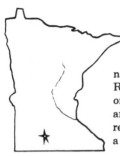

WATONWAN COUNTY once had a hero schoolteacher named George A. Bradford. He taught 16 pupils in Riverdale township. A blizzard struck in the afternoon of January 7, 1873. Bradford kept his charges in school— and he kept them there until well into the third day when rescuers finally got through. That blizzard of '73 is still a topic of conversation.

New Year's Eggnog Pie

1 baked pastry shell
4 egg yolks, slightly beaten
½ cup sugar
½ teaspoon salt
½ cup hot water
¼ cup cold water
1 tablespoon unflavored gelatin
4 egg whites, stiffly beaten
½ cup sugar
1 teaspoon nutmeg
2 teaspoons rum

Cook first 4 ingredients over boiling water, stirring constantly, until mixture coats a spoon. Soak gelatin in the cold water for 5 minutes. Pour custard over gelatin mixture, blend well and cool.

When mixture starts to congeal, fold in stiffly-beaten egg whites, blended with sugar, nutmeg, and rum. Pour mixture into a baked pie shell and chill until firm. If you wish, spread with thin layer of whipped cream and sprinkle with nutmeg before serving. This recipe will fill a crust made in 9" pie tin.

Giftas

Cook 1 quart cranberries until soft in water to cover. Add 1½ cups sugar. Stir well. Pour into bowl and cool. Keep in refrigerator while making following: Crush 1½ dozen graham crackers or cinnamon rusks (add a little salt to crumbs). Whip stiff 1½ cups heavy cream. Place in a glass bowl alternate layers of crumbs, cranberries, and whipped cream. Garnish with design of whole cooked cranberries and whipped cream.

Fresh Peach Delight

Graham cracker crust
16 marshmallows
½ cup milk
¾ cup cream, whipped
1½ cups fresh peaches, diced
1 tablespoon sugar
½ teaspoon vanilla

Melt marshmallows in milk over medium heat. Cool. Add whipped cream, mixed with sugar, vanilla, and peaches. Pour into a graham cracker crust and top with graham cracker crumbs. Refrigerate for at least 1 hour before serving.

Mint Snowballs

1 cup shortening
½ cup powdered sugar
2 teaspoons water
½ teaspoon salt
2 cups sifted flour
1 cup quick oatmeal

Bake 25 to 30 minutes at 350 degrees. Frost and roll in shredded coconut.

Frosting

2 cups powdered sugar
½ teaspoon mint extract
¼ cup milk
Green food coloring

Ground Brazil Nut Cookies

1 cup butter
⅔ cup sugar
1 egg
1 teaspoon vanilla
1¾ cups flour
½ teaspoon salt
1½ cups Brazil nuts, ground

Cream butter and sugar, add egg and vanilla. Mix ground nuts with flour and salt and add to creamed mixture. Bake in 400 degree oven.

WILKIN COUNTY named itself three times and twice changed its mind. When it was organized in 1858, the name was Toombs, after a senator from Georgia. When he deserted the Union, the settlers switched to Andy Johnson. When Johnson became unpopular, the county honored Alexander Wilkin, St. Paul lawyer killed in the Civil war.

Czechoslovakian Cookies

3½ cups sifted flour
½ pound butter
½ teaspoon salt
2 egg yolks
1 whole egg
½ pint sour cream
1 cake yeast dissolved in warm water
1 teaspoon vanilla

Mix flour, butter, and salt together like pie crust. Add yolks and whole egg, then sour cream, yeast and water, and vanilla. Mix together and put in refrigerator for 2 hours. Roll out thin on a sugared board and cut into 1½" squares. Put about 1 teaspoon filling in center of each square. Overlap 2 ends, leaving 2 ends open. Bake at 350 degrees 12 to 15 minutes.

Filling

1½ cups Grapenuts
¼-½ cup sugar
⅛ cup melted butter
Little cinnamon

Christmas Shortbread from Canada

1 cup butter
½ cup powdered sugar
1 egg
¼ teaspoon salt
2 cups flour (about)

Soften butter slightly but do not allow it to become oily. Stir in sugar, salt, and egg yolk, using wooden spoon. Add flour, a very little at a time, until mixture is too stiff to work with spoon.

Turn onto floured board and knead lightly, drawing in flour all the time until the dough "just begins to crack." Roll out to ¼" thickness. Shape or cut into fancy cookies, such as bells, trees, stars, etc. Decorate with almonds or cherries if desired. Bake at 325 degrees until a delicate brown. Allow to cool in pan.

Meat Ball One-course Dinner

1 pound ground beef
½ pound ground pork
1 cup tomato soup
1 tablespoon flour
¾ teaspoon salt
¼ teaspoon pepper
1 cup mushrooms, fresh or canned, cut up
1 cup onions, chopped
2 cups celery, diced
4 cups potatoes, cut up
1 teaspoon salt

Mix ground beef, ground pork, tomato soup, flour, salt, and pepper; shape into small balls about 1½" in diameter. Brown in frying pan. Arrange meat balls in bottom of roaster and cover with remaining ingredients. Cover and bake 50 to 60 minutes at 350 degrees or cook on top of stove on low heat.

Three Layer Bars

½ cup butter
½ cup sugar
5 tablespoons cocoa
1 teaspoon vanilla
1 egg, beaten
2 cups graham cracker crumbs
1 cup coconut
½ cup nutmeats

Cook butter, sugar, and cocoa in double boiler to a thin custard. Add vanilla and egg; then add graham cracker crumbs, coconut, and nutmeats. Pack into 9" x 9" pan.

Spread mixture of following ingredients over first layer:

¼ cup butter
2 tablespoons vanilla pudding powder
2 tablespoons milk
2 cups sifted powdered sugar

Top with following and then refrigerate and cut into very small bars for serving.

4-5 squares semi-sweet chocolate,
melted with
1 tablespoon butter

WINONA COUNTY was hunting grounds for the Sioux until Winona, the county seat, was founded in 1851. A lumber boom followed settlement of Winona, and today the city rests on tons of sawdust reinforcing the sands of the Mississippi river bank. Winona's famed Sugar Loaf mountain was once a burial site for the Sioux. They hung their dead on open racks at the foot of the mountain.

Boiled (or Poached) Fish with Burned Butter Sauce

Use only lean fish such as pike, sheepshead, whitefish, perch, or catfish. Fat fish is better baked. Use whole fish if possible. Wrap in cheesecloth or fine muslin. Start cooking in very cold, salted broth, bring to a boil, skim, reduce heat and start counting 6 to 8 minutes a pound while simmering. Do not overcook and do not pierce with a fork to see if it is done. You can tell more by timing. When done, remove to a hot platter, remove top skin and pour over burned butter sauce.

Broth (Court-bouillon)

⅔ to 1 cup vinegar

2 quarts cold water

1 tablespoon salt

2 small carrots, thinly sliced

2 medium-sized onions, thinly sliced

1 teaspoon cracked pepper, or peppercorns

2 whole cloves

2 bay leaves

½ teaspoon thyme

Bring to boil, then simmer for 20 minutes. Strain and set aside to cool. One quart white or red wine and 1 quart water may be substituted for first 2 ingredients.

Burned Butter Sauce

Chop 1 shallot or a tablespoon of chives or minced onion. Put in saucepan with ½ cup cold water and 2 tablespoons of vinegar, with salt and pepper to taste. Reduce over a hot fire until about half in volume and vinegar smells almost burned. Keep hot without boiling and add very gradually, a little bit at a time, ½ pound butter, stirring and rocking the mixture, until each piece of butter is absorbed. Should be foamy. Pour over boiled fish.

Tough Venison Roast

When young and tender, venison should be cooked as one would the finest lean beef. But when old, it may be tough. It is best to marinate it for 8 hours, turning frequently, in the following marinade:

> 1 large onion
> 4 cloves
> 1 cup tarragon vinegar
> 2 carrots, chopped
> 2 teaspoons pickling or shrimp spice
> 5 tablespoons oil
> Lots of salt and pepper

Remove the meat and insert slivers of garlic and rosemary. Place slivers of ginger over the top. If possible to use side meat, top with slices of this after salting. If necessary, use salt pork to top and then use no salt. Do not use bacon unless you prefer the taste of bacon to venison. The fat meat will help baste the venison. Cover and cook at 300 degrees until a meat thermometer shows beef as you like it—rare, medium or well done. Or figure 16, 22 or 30 minutes per pound for rare, medium or well done. Occasionally uncover and pour on some of the marinade, as long as it lasts.

St. Patrick's Cake

This cake should be made at least a week before it is served.

> 1 egg, well beaten
> 1 cup brown sugar
> ¾ cup dark molasses
> 1 teaspoon cloves, ground
> ½ cup fat salt pork, ground fine
> ½ cup dried currants
> 1 cup nutmeats, chopped
> 1 cup strong black coffee
> 1 teaspoon soda
> 1 teaspoon cinnamon
> ¼ teaspoon nutmeg
> ½ pound seedless raisins
> 3 ounces dried citron
> 2 cups flour

Beat eggs well, mix in coffee, sugar, soda, molasses, cinnamon, cloves, and nutmeg. Mix in finely-ground pork. Using wooden spoon, stir in the raisins, currants, citron, and nutmeats. Sift in flour gradually, stirring until all is thoroughly mixed. Bake at 300 degrees about 1 hour.

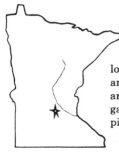

WRIGHT COUNTY has more than 400 lakes, temptingly located as a lure to Twin Cities residents. The lakes around Annandale and Buffalo, in particular, are important resort centers. Indians found the area rich in wild game and fish. Its devotees today claim it just as rich for pike, bass, sunfish and crappie fishing.

Shrimp Casserole

1 cup milk, scalded
⅔ cup bread crumbs
3 tablespoons melted butter
2 tablespoons pimiento, chopped
1 tablespoon onion, chopped
1 cup American cheese, grated
2 eggs, beaten
¼ teaspoon salt
Dash pepper
⅔ to 1 cup cooked or canned vegetables, drained
1 can shrimp

Pour scalded milk over bread crumbs; add butter, pimiento, onion, cheese, eggs, and seasonings. Place vegetable and drained shrimp in greased 1½-quart casserole. Pour milk and cheese mixture over them. Set in pan of warm water and bake about 1¼ hours, or until firm, at 325 degrees. Serves 4.

Bread Pudding

12 slices dry bread, cut into small pieces
4 eggs
4 cups sweet milk
¾ cup white sugar
½ teaspoon salt
Nutmeg or lemon juice to taste

Beat slightly and add all ingredients to cut-up bread. Bake about 1 hour in slow oven (250 degrees) with baking dish placed in hot water. Serve with any drained fruit or hard sauce.

Marshmallow Chocolate Cake

¼ pound marshmallows
2 squares chocolate, grated
½ cup hot water
1½ cups sifted cake flour
1 teaspoon soda
1 teaspoon salt
2 eggs, beaten
1 cup sugar
1 cup sour cream
1 teaspoon vanilla

Melt marshmallows and chocolate in double boiler. Add hot water, beating to smooth paste. Cool. Sift flour, measure, sift again with soda and salt. Beat eggs, add sugar, whip until creamy. Add sour cream; stir until smooth. Fold flour mixture gradually into egg mixture. Carefully fold in chocolate-marshmallow paste and vanilla. Turn batter into 2 greased layer cake pans and bake 30 to 35 minutes at 375 degrees. Frost with a chocolate frosting.

Mock Angel Food Cake

1 cup sugar
1½ cups flour
2 teaspoons baking powder
½ teaspoon salt
1 teaspoon vanilla
1 cup scalded milk
2 egg whites, beaten stiff

Mix sugar, flour, baking powder, salt, and vanilla; pour over scalded milk. Fold in egg whites. Bake in ungreased pan at 350 degrees for about 50 minutes.

Macaroni Fruit Salad

¾ cup uncooked macaroni
3 bananas, chopped
3 oranges, chopped
15 marshmallows, chopped
1 No. 2 can pineapple, drained

Cook macaroni, drain and blanch. Add remaining ingredients and mix with dressing.

Dressing
½ cup sugar
1 egg yolk
Pineapple juice

Make a smooth paste; cook over hot water until thickened. Cool.

YELLOW MEDICINE COUNTY'S official records once resided in a haystack. It was in the days when Granite Falls and the vanished village of Yellow Medicine were battling for county seat. A Granite Falls posse seized the records and kept them hidden until their town won an 1876 court suit. The records reappeared at once.

Applesauce Fruit Cake

    3 cups hot applesauce
    1 cup shortening
    2 cups sugar
4½ cups flour
    4 teaspoons soda
    1 teaspoon nutmeg
    1 teaspoon salt
3½ teaspoons cinnamon
    ½ teaspoon cloves
    1 teaspoon allspice
    1 pound light raisins
    1 pound dark raisins
    1 pound mixed fruit peel
    Walnuts

Add shortening and sugar to applesauce and let stand overnight. Sift flour and spices together three times. Add to overnight mixture along with remaining ingredients. Bake at 325 degrees for about 3 hours.

Raspberry Roll-ups

    1 cup butter
    1 8-ounce package cream cheese
    2 cups flour
    ½ teaspoon salt
    Raspberry jam

Mix all ingredients and roll dough 1 6" thick. Cut into 2½" squares. Put 1 teaspoon raspberry jam on each square and spread, not too close to edges. Roll firmly and bake on ungreased tin until golden brown (about 12 minutes) at 425 degrees.

Spaghetti Loaf

1½ cups uncooked spaghetti, broken up
1 cup milk
4 tablespoons butter
3 eggs, separated
1 generous cup grated cheese
  (cream, Edam, or other)
¾ cup bread crumbs
1 teaspoon onion, grated
1 teaspoon pimiento, chopped
½ teaspoon salt
¼ teaspoon pepper

Cook spaghetti until tender. Heat milk to scalding and add butter. When melted, pour over beaten egg yolks. Add cheese, crumbs, and remaining ingredients. Fold beaten egg whites into mixture and bake 1 hour at 350 degrees, lowering to 325 degrees the last half hour. Bake in well-buttered mold set in boiling water.

Over this pour sauce made from 1 can cream of tomato soup, ½ cup cream heated to boiling point. (Do not boil.)

Old-fashioned Ginger Molasses Cake

½ cup sugar
½ cup shortening
2 eggs
½ cup dark molasses
½ cup sour milk, with 1 teaspoon
  soda added
½ cup strong black coffee (cold)
1 teaspoon cinnamon
1 teaspoon nutmeg
1 teaspoon cloves
1 teaspoon salt
2 cups raisins, previously soaked
  in hot water
½ cup nut meats
2 cups plus 2 tablespoons flour

Bake in small loaf pans 1 hour at 350 degrees.

INDEX

SAUCES, Dessert and Meat

SOUP

SPECIALTIES

SUPPER DISHES

VEGETABLES